GR/W

Careers
in the
Music Business

CW01551778

Careers
in the
Music Business

Hilary Hayward

Kogan
Page

First published 1983 by Kogan Page Ltd
120 Pentonville Road, London N1 9JN

British Library Cataloguing in Publication Data

Hayward, Hilary
    Careers in the music business.—(Kogan Page
    careers series)
    1. Music, Popular (songs, etc.)—Vocational guidance
    I. Title
    780'.42   ML3545

    ISBN 0-85038-609-8 (Hb)
    ISBN 0-85038-610-1 (Pb)

Printed in Great Britain by The Anchor Press Ltd
Tiptree, Essex

Contents

Part 2

Part 1
Introduction

The Music Business

There's only one person in the music industry. He's mean, self-interested and self-seeking, greedy, over-ambitious and as tough as old boots. He has the disposition of a despot and the sharp-edged business brain of a boomerang — a primitive if sometimes lethal weapon. The old adage that it's a business fit only for young men is wrong — you can keep going just as long as your heart holds out, assuming that your wits haven't been dulled by too many hotel breakfasts and night club cocktails. If this happens — watch out — skid row is always just around the corner. The world is full of butchers and postmen who once put their noses in the music industry oven without first bothering to check the temperature control setting. Of course if you are one of the lucky people whose skin consists of a fine, heat resistant india-rubber substance, then you'll probably survive. Or you may have an inherited family estate to retire to when the fun is over!

It should be said here that not everyone's in it just for the money. Some people have so much musical talent, not necessarily in terms of skill in playing an instrument or singing, but also in judging the public taste at an exact moment, in recognising talent and knowing the right way to exploit it without killing it off too quickly, that they would be wasting their lives in any other industry. What's the point of working in a baked bean factory if the only thing that really moves you is a Bruce Springsteen concert? If there was an A level in enthusiasm, you'd need to score top marks in the S level paper to qualify for even the lowliest of positions — and that means more enthusiasm and belief in yourself than carries most people through their job interviews. It means enough high-spirited confidence to carry you through black, poverty-stricken years, knowing that you'll make it in the end. When that wears out and cynicism begins to creep in, then give up and go back to the baked bean factory.

How to Enter

Lots of people ask, 'How do I get into the music business?' as if there's some kind of garden wall they have to climb over to enter that secret society who, as seen on television, all drive round in black limousines, wear flamboyant clothes, and have beautiful partners at their sides. But the beauty of the entertainment world as a whole is that it's open to any Tom, Dick or Francesca who wants to have a go and has a product worth selling. There *is* an old boy network, nurtured by all those who have passed the 'we've made it through the rain' test, but they only control a few jobs — the biggest employer is the public, who pays the wages, pays for the limousines and all the fun. In return he is able (subject to media pre-programming) to spend his leisure money on exactly what he likes. If you can persuade him that your product is just what he wants, then the old boys will have to come to you — as they will — because they know that the rules of survival don't include pride, only good business sense. Remember that when you sell the publishing rights of your artist to pay the phone bill, and he turns out to be Elvis Presley II!

Following the Fortunes of a Band

So now let's follow the fortunes of a small four-piece rock band who have recognisable talent and are playing something just a little different, although at the moment it's only from the garage of the bass player's house. They're all young, having just left school with a few CSEs and school reports which complain mainly of time taken off to rehearse — will it all be worth it? Two of them have been lucky enough to find jobs — one working in a shop and the other as a petrol pump attendant — but the other two have signed on the dole, and are spending their time sitting in each other's bedrooms writing songs and feeling fairly miserable. In the end, sheer boredom drives them out to a few of the local pubs to ask the landlords if they would consider allowing the band to play there. To their delight and amazement, charm wins through and they obtain their first couple of gigs. The landlord of one of the pubs seems enthusiastic about them, and gives them a regular weekly spot during the resident dj's evening break. This encourages them to pool their total gig earnings in a building society account in order to save up for a proper set of equipment. Live work is just what their music needs — just a few months of gigging sees a vast improvement in their stage presence, and the lead singer's voice.

Their confidence improves eventually to the point where they feel ready to make a tape, and send it off to anybody who might be able to help them on their road to certain (as they see it) stardom. Deciding to make a proper job of this, they take every last penny out of their building society account and go into an eight-track studio late one night to cut four songs, with the aid of a friendly engineer whom they've plied with beer and taken along to a gig. The result isn't bad, not perhaps quite what they'd hoped for, but they have made as many copies as they can afford and sent them off to other venues, further afield. These include: a few small London ones, some agents, a few a & r men in record companies (talent scouts) and even one to a friendly-sounding writer on *Sounds*. They send accompanying letters explaining who they are, and include a rather blurred photo of themselves taken in the local park. This they follow closely up with visits and phone calls, resulting in a few tentatively encouraging words in *Sounds*, and one or two London gigs which a few agents and a & r men promise faithfully to attend. Actually only a couple of them show up to the first night, which is just as well because the bass player gets drunk early on in the evening and blows the set.

One of the agents offers to try and get them a few gigs around the colleges, and they agree to let him do so, though not before they sack the bass player.His place is soon filled by another young bass player who adds a new, slightly funkier edge to their music and the gigging goes on.

Eventually the band release their first single via a local independent record company, and it sounds nothing like the first eager demonstration tape which now seems like something produced in another age. The single enters the independent charts, and the agent suddenly finds booking work for the band an easy task. Their audiences swell and a fan club is begun locally, handled by the lead singer's girl-friend. Then one night after a particularly good gig a man approaches them backstage and offers to manage them. He already handles a few other bands quite well and has those all-important contacts within record companies to secure them a good deal.

They agree, and within six months they've got a record deal, signed after no less than three major companies have put in varying bids. One offered a huge advance with almost no royalties, another a small advance but good royalties and a hard-working, enthusiastic team and the third offered them a wage but guaranteed huge success if they would only dress the same and record the songs of a well-known writing duo. The last company assured them that their fortunes would be made by the vast amount of world-wide personal appearances on radio and television, after their first smash hit single. They opt for the middle company on the wise advice of their manager, who also has arranged for them to go out on tour supporting a well-known band at the same time as their first proper single release.

A year later they've made their first album and are a household name with adoring fans following them around the world. They have enough money in the bank to set up their own independent record label and help other bands like themselves. They own a 16-track studio with a rehearsal room complex in the basement, so that their incomes are assured long after their chart success fades. The lead guitarist, in fact, starts to produce bands that come through the studio and before long has made a name for himself as an excellent producer.

Some Advice

Obviously there are many bands whose story is completely different from that outlined here. It takes some musicians 10 or 12 years before any kind of success comes to them, and sometimes a band must go through a hundred line-up changes before it eventually hits the right combination. But talent and persistence always win out in the end. A loser is entirely of his own making, but a winner needs not only his own strength and support but also that of an experienced manager, agent, record company.

Regarding the publishing rights on a group's songs, an experienced manager will either have made them keep their own publishing rights, handled by himself, or will have sold them off to a well-reputed company to look after, so that they don't lose out on all that extra easy income. When success comes it brings its own special kind of problems: chasing up royalties paid in obscure countries where the product is selling well, investing money wisely (nowadays no one is stupid enough to see his success as particularly everlasting), handling the non-stop round of press interviews (for which a good press officer is a must), organising a tour which will reap maximum effect in terms of exposure and record sales, and making sure that the sound, lighting and stage show are new, fresh and perfect on each night. For this last a whole team of experts in these fields is necessary. Finally you must make sure that you have enough time to yourself both to write new, interesting material and to keep recording successful albums. If the public interest in your music wanes at any stage, you will be amazed how quickly your support teams collapse around you — leaving you alone with your gold discs and CSEs.

The focal pivot of the music industry is the musician. The whole aim and object of the exercise is to sell records. Cynical record company executives, who should know better, call them simply 'units of product'; they prefer to leave the creativity to the artist and producer. As far as the public is concerned, it wants to see and to hear its favourite band, whether live, on record, or in the media. All the myriad jobs and small businesses, which abound in the entertainment world, have grown out of the success of the artist. They depend for their livelihood on the enthusiasm of the public for anything to do with that artist.

Chapter 1
The Musician

Introduction

There aren't any statistics available about the number of musicians around who are barely earning a living — and have been barely doing so for many years — compared to the number who are living the life of a millionaire. Musicians today are like the actors of Shakespeare's day — second class citizens expected by society to produce greater and greater forms of their art without any kind of financial return. The top few per cent may earn a fabulous living for a short while, and a miniscule percentage of that few may continue to earn millions for the rest of their lives, but any aspiring musician should confidently expect to remain in the majority — there's no point in planning otherwise.

A utopian society would admit its need for entertainment — popular or otherwise — and would support saxophonists, drummers, guitarists, violinists, regardless of whether they sold a million records or not. Unfortunately we don't live in an ideal society. Young musicians are forced to work by day and practise their music at night in garages, at local discos and public houses. Why don't the influential people in the music industry do more to encourage young musicians? The fact is, they won't take the risk. Many youngsters have potential, but it's always difficult to know whose potential is going to develop into a real talent.

Even when a musician has become well known, his problems are not over. His public thinks that it has a right to expect a steady, consistent output from him, and if it doesn't receive this it may withdraw its support. After years spent in satisfying the public's taste rather than his own, a

13

musician may become worn out, with all his former talent spent.

Music whether it be classical, pop, or punk is important, perhaps it's something that society as a whole takes too much for granted.

To Train or not to Train?

Musical training, both in school and in college, is almost exclusively towards a classical career (no less insecure) which takes into account for the most part the 'great Masters' — mainly European musicians and composers — such as: Handel, Tchaikovsky, Mendelssohn, Bach, etc. If you want to learn ancient African rhythms you'll probably have to look elsewhere. The best way to learn is through your own favourite musician — musicians are prepared to help each other to an enormous degree. This does not mean that you should ring up Eric Clapton to ask him to teach you to play the guitar (you could learn his style from his records), but musicians help each other by exchanging influences and experiences, which all agree help to develop their own personal style. The session musician is often frustrated when he goes into a recording studio and is asked to 'play in the style of so and so . . .' The so and so mentioned is as likely as not to be famous just because he has his own personal, distinctive style which has taken him years of learning and listening to perfect.

Famous percussionists in this country, when asked how they've learnt their incredible rhythms, will to a man tell you that they travelled to their country of origin with an open mind and a willingness to learn, to watch the great African or South American masters of rhythm at work. Or they've at least worked alongside another musician who has done just that. It's important to remember that all music stems from another kind — it helps to understand the music that influences you most while you are learning. There's no shame in learning to begin with to sing, dance or play an instrument in exactly the style of one of your heroes — the most famous artists will admit to beginning that way —

because as you progress and develop, your own personality and style will begin to come through. You will undoubtedly achieve something stronger and more positive than the style you began with.

The culture is there for you — all you have to do is not be afraid to take advantage of it. One of the positive aspects of music is that it is without pretension or class structure, if you have the talent, then you also have the power. A certain amount of academia in music would be an excellent idea, but not so much that its feel is lost for ever in a welter of books and musical notes. Music springs from the soul, not the brain, you'll be glad to hear, and the more it opens itself to diverse influences the stronger it becomes. You may have lived in an air bubble at the bottom of the sea, gaining your influences from the dolphins — you have something to contribute. Come out of your air bubble, listen to the sounds around you that most excite your senses, and adapt your music to suit your feelings. Musicians on the outside will in turn benefit from you —that's how it works. Don't be in a hurry to become an overnight success — it won't benefit your music in the long run.

If you've had a one-off hit with a song at the age of 19, you may be regretting it at the age of 40, when you're playing it for the millionth time. Bob Dylan admits that his sixties adulation was a mixture of heaven and hell for him — the journalists browsing his dustbins were hell, as was the stifling attitude of his fans who still expected him to play 20 years later 'Blowing in the Wind' note for note as it first appeared (while he was a teenager), booing him off stage if he tried to play anything new. Guitar heroes who laid down a timeless riff in a moment of inspiration during a studio session, have since lived to regret their genius, as they churn out the same notes in the same place during the song their band are still being forced to play 10 years later. A few notes changed, a note held longer, may improve the song, but leave the audience unconvinced.

Where Can You Practise?

It would be encouraging to imagine a scenario in 10 or 20 years' time where musicians' workshops are the norm — rather like actors' workshops, where weekends or entire weeks are given over to artists getting together, talking about music, playing it, teaching others and learning from each other — the conservatories of Vienna taking place in Brixton and Hounslow. It happens very occasionally now — mainly in the jazz world (Cleo Laine and Johnny Dankworth are much to be praised for their work with jazz workshops for young people, but they can't benefit everyone) — and it should happen more. There should be somewhere musicians could go to during the evening, the weekend, or even during the day, and meet other musicians, maybe even famous ones who are taking time off between tours and albums and public appearances to engulf themselves in a thriving, constructive musical atmosphere.

Until then, you must rely on the indulgence of your parents who allow you to make a noise in your bedroom or garage with like-minded friends, or your school who might be persuaded to provide extra-curricular space in an outhouse — hardly condusive to creativity, you may imagine, but it's better than nothing if you are sufficiently enthusiastic. If you don't have a youth club in your area, then approach the local vicar for the use of his church hall, or the local council for the use of some otherwise unoccupied hall for somewhere to go at least one night each week. Here you could set up your instruments and play for your local community and even charge enough money on the door to cover p.a (public address) hire for the night, if you think that's a possibility. A few years ago lots of bands began that way, but a bureaucratic refusal to understand the 'need' for available venues for teenagers below the drinking age has made the hiring of suitable places very difficult.

Finding a Manager

If you want to go up the next step of the ladder, you'll need a manager. This may be a dynamic friend with time to spare, or it may be a member of the band who has the right personality to handle it — read Chapter 2, The Manager, for further information on the right personality. You'll stay in your church hall unless someone is prepared to take time selling you out of it, into some proper venues. Success won't ever come to you — you have to go and seek it out for yourself. If you're good and you know it — get someone presentable and articulate out in the streets and into peoples offices, telling them all about you.

Marketing Aids

Marketing aids are invaluable here, those people in their offices, or managing their venues, are only too used to being approached by enthusiastic managers. You have to find something slightly different, which will make them listen. A non-aggressive approach helps. The essense of good marketing is not to arouse the anger of your prey before you can get in too close. Too many bands send tapes through the post, to journalists, radio djs like John Peel and record company a & r men, without any concept or understanding that their tape is just one in a pile of 20 received that week, all of which may have something to offer. Do not telephone the recipient of your tape after only a few days, and demand to know what he thought of it. Being impatient, irritable or rude will not benefit you at all, and it might actually harm your tape's chances.

If you want to 'go public' with yourselves, you'll have to be prepared to sacrifice a few tapes for good, a few good 'usable' photographs and a bit of shoe-leather, as the direct approach is by far the most effective, assuming that you are the sociable type. You are in competition with hundreds of others, just as if you were applying for a sought-after job. You should approach people in the music industry as you would a prospective employer, not as if they owed you a living. Every single person in the music industry is entirely self-made, and has worked very hard to get there all by himself. As long as the music business continues to be structured on the 'survival of the fittest' theory, it will be expected, rightly, that you should be the same. If you aren't one of the 'fittest' but you are a talented musician, then it's all the more important to find a manager who will go out there and do your surviving for you.

Making Your Own Record

Another marketing aid which is fast becoming invaluable in this day and age is some product of your own (see Chapter 4 on independent record companies). There may be a small record company in your area who can be persuaded to come and watch you play, or hear your tape and thus put out some product for you. This will do a great deal in terms of convincing those around you that you really do exist musically. As regards your image, there's something very concrete about a piece of black vinyl, and it's much more likely to get heard by the people you most want to influence. It also provides you with the excellent experience of going into a recording studio and undergoing the discipline of putting your ideas down onto something solid. When it's in its finished form, put it on your record player among a few of your favourite records. Does it reach their standards, professionally?

Your approach to the studio concept is something you have to work out for yourself — it's nothing like playing live, where the occasional slip-up can go unnoticed in a frenzy of raw excitement. The studio is much more discerning. The joy of the very early rock 'n' roll records is that bands went into studios and recreated their fresh, live sound without all the technology that is available today to help them. An independent single — even as a one-off on your own specially created label — is a powerful weapon in your armoury, including your emotional one. It's very hard to stand slightly apart from what you are doing and give an accurate assessment — you may be so closely involved with yourself that you end up losing a concept of reality, or your place within the current music scene. It's useful to have someone around you who can always give an honest opinion of your worth.

The Chart System

Don't forget that the music industry is very fashion-conscious. Your music may have a place in the popular charts of 10 years ahead. If you believe in it enough, that shouldn't worry you too much, and, fortunately for you, there are at least 20 different record-buying markets, some of whom still want to hear Vera Lynn and some of whom haven't finished learning the words of 'Baa Baa Black Sheep' yet. This is why there are so many different kinds of charts these days: one for the heavy metal fans, one for the 'pop pickers', one for the disco fans, one for the reggae fans and one for the musical intelligensia, the Indie charts. Most are meaningless — only a placing in the British Market Research Bureau's charts will guarantee television exposure although this by no means indicates that you are the most popular artist around at the moment — the BMRB charts are compiled from sales figures of a few selected record shops around the country. These are shops which you may never even have visited but which are very carefully looked after by the major record companies, who know exactly where they are.

You may have heard the term chart 'hyping' which caused such a scandal a few years back when the major record companies were accused of manipulating the lower end of the BMRB chart to their own purposes. Their belief was that once the record found its way into that end of the chart, the BBC who actively support the chart, would lend its 'establishment' stamp of approval, by playing the records on their nationwide programmes, and thus send them shooting up to the Top Twenty and fame. But this chart is almost as meaningless as the others now, although they are all a good indication of the popularity of a song. If you compared actual sales figures, however, of various singles, you may now and again find that one that hasn't gone into the BMRB chart — possibly it's reggae, punk, or independent — has found its way to the top of one of the other charts, but is still ignored by the BBC mainstream programmes. It may have sold more, but it's still minority to the music establishment until the BMRB chart says otherwise. Fortunately, after all the furore of publicity given to 'hyping', the BBC abolished its chart-linked playlist. This has given record programme producers much more freedom regarding the playing of records they consider worthy of note, whether they appear in the charts or not, and has gone a long way towards opening up the music scene, and steering it out of the hands of a privileged few.

Success and after

Just a few words on the total inadvisability of going on a spending spree the minute your income starts rolling in. If you or your manager has negotiated a record or publishing deal that pays a large advance, try and avoid the temptation of the sports cars and the expensive life-style which can eat away an advance before you've had time to record the first album. The time to spend money is *after* your first album has started to become successful. The advance is there to further your career; it should be invested to that end. When a record or publishing company has shown their faith in you by producing their cheque books, they're saying, 'Now go out and prove to us that you're worth it'. An advance should be just enough to cover new equipment, if it's needed, studio time (if they haven't offered to pay for it), and enough to keep you all alive for the duration. If you can keep the advance small enough to cover all that, without going on a spending spree, then you can undoubtedly negotiate a better slice of the final product for yourselves — a better share in the proceeds of record sales which is, after all, the object of the exercise. Many acts think that once they've signed up with a record company for the largest advance they can negotiate, the job's over. Of course it's not — the battle has just begun. There are many acts who've supposedly been the next 'big' thing, signed after huge cheque book battles between the major record companies, only to sink into total obscurity within two or three failed singles, a marathon effort by the promotions department, and several expensive videos.

Even with a few hyped singles behind you, if you haven't got what it takes, the public will soon realise it. A good plan of action to pursue when several companies are beginning to show an interest is to sign a publishing deal. It works in almost the same way as a record deal, including an advance which may actually outweigh that of a record company. If you sign a publishing deal you may find yourself with enough money in your pocket to invest in your act sufficiently — perhaps even producing an independent single — and improving it to the point where you have a really saleable commodity to offer the record companies. The eventual deal you negotiate as a result is likely to be much more to your advantage than it would otherwise have been. Some publishing companies will actually negotiate your record deal for you, after all it's in their interest for you to be on record, as they can't earn any money from you until then (they'll be taking a percentage of the record sales). They'll also look after your royalties quite carefully, which is where many record companies are found to be lacking, particularly as regards those hard-to-trace overseas earnings.

If you really start earning a fortune, remember you're in the music business now — it's your chosen career.If you're still young, then you'll have to do some fast growing up and acquire some business sense quickly. What will you do when the money stops coming? You may still be a genius, but the public may have moved on to something new. If you are sensible, you'll have launched a management company, an independent record company, a recording studio, or even a p.a. hire company. The Jam, for example, own Respond Records, now doing very well under the auspices of Paul Weller while he's not writing or touring. Gallagher and Lyle owned their own p.a. system and started a small business with it, hiring it out to other bands while they weren't touring. It's now a thriving p.a. hire company, overseen by their sound engineer, which will guarantee them an income for many years to come.

The music industry is full of wise musicians who have moved into 'desk jobs' long after their own musical careers are over. Many manage new exciting acts who are hits in their own right — for example Adam Faith manages Leo Sayer — others work as a & r men, record company executives or famous producers. As musicians, they know that they have to stay emotionally close to the business as long as they live, and they also know that it can be as exciting to manage or produce a band as it is to be in one themselves, and more financially stable. Nearly all the major names you can think of have thriving companies of their own which will continue long after their demise.

Case Study

If you've been expecting a famous pop or rock star here, forget it. If you want to read their stories, you can do so in the musical press. This is the story of a 26-year old musician who has been in the music business all his working life but is not yet famous. *Dave Bitelli* is a fabulous, undiscovered musician who lives and breathes — almost literally — his saxophone. Not only can he not put a note wrong, but his ability to communicate through his music is so powerful that it's impossible for anyone not to be affected by his playing. His father was strongly against his entry into the music business. He had watched his own father struggle against poverty as a professional violinist, so it's not surprising that he didn't want Dave to suffer similarly. But if you've got music in your blood you just can't ignore it, and by his late teens Dave was living in a squat in London, trying to earn his living playing the saxophone.

He went to music college eventually which didn't impress him over much, although he now says with hindsight that he was influenced by and is indebted to several of the teachers there, whom he wishes were still available to him. One advantage of music college is that it allows you time to practise. The small grants are a definite disadvantage.

He claims to be still learning, although he does a few sessions. He toured America as a part of Joe N Jackson's Jumping Jive venture recently, and he has played alongside a few of the great masters of music. At the moment he is exercising his great passion for Latin-American influenced salsa music, with an eight-piece band behind him called the Onward Internationals. His only problem is keeping them out of other hit acts long enough for them to release a single and go on tour together.

Music is one of my big pleasures in life; I love playing my saxophone. I think I'm very lucky to be able to earn my living doing something that I enjoy so much. It's just a pity that the music business is so full of rip-offs; the people that control the purse-strings are basically idiots who know nothing about music. To obtain a gig in a restaurant, for example, you may find yourself dealing with the catering manager, which is depressing, to say the least. But there are musicians who are just as bad: session musicians standing around in studios with a stop-watch in one hand, caring nothing about the actual music they're helping to make, nor being interested enough to invest in a good musical venture with some of their own time and money. You also come across dance band musicians who don't care about what the people want to dance to they've got their set, and they play it without deviation or enthusiasm. They're killing music themselves by their attitudes, and they all deserve to be extinct.

Good musicians don't have to sell out commercially. There's a difference between compromising and selling out, you just have to be versatile. Even in the various pubs and clubs where I play around London, I find myself playing the same music in a totally different way, according to what I feel the audience wants from me. I've played in some bands where we simply did the same 60-minute show every night, but to survive, I feel that you really do have to be more versatile than that. In the same way, if you play a big stadium, you have to play a show that goes with it.

I don't like the way the pop industry has developed as regards touring — it's become such a hyped, mammoth operation — catering, lighting, p.a. and trucking companies all cruising around in luxury coaches, it's got completely out of hand. I would like to see a return to the situation where a band just goes out there and plays with the minimum of fuss and hype. It can be done, as bands like Morrissey Mullen have proved, they are always working, whether or not they have an album to promote. They simply book themselves into a hall with a certain capacity, work out a ticket price to cover their overheads (which are minimal) and some salary, and everyone comes out happy — they're really popular on the live circuit. Playing to people is a form of communication. I enjoy playing my horn, but I'm also trying to reach some sort of oneness with the audience; this has to be worked at, I have to try to hit the right wavelength. If the musicians have worked hard enough and the people listening appreciate and understand what they're trying to express, then that's great — it makes it all worthwhile.

I'm basically trying to play the best tunes and rhythms I can — that is to say the strongest, the least watered down. I feel I'm talking to the world when I'm playing, although it's not really me as such — I'm serving up what's already there. People have been doing this same thing for literally thousands of years, I'm just plugging in to that particular stream of culture. I'm not around to do sensational pyrotechnics on my instrument. I don't have any ambitions to be the fastest saxophone player, or to play the best changes — that's not my thing but I can be strong, heartfelt and I can move people, I hope to make my living by being that good for people. I believe there's a place for music in society, just as there's a place for the man who drives a bus.

I'm a member of the Musicians' Union. The MU is great where large businesses are concerned, without its interven-tion on behalf of individual musicians, we would be regularly walked all over. If there was no MU then musicians would almost have to pay to appear on radio or television, whereas the situation now is that it's very well paid. Musicians are rather like actors — they're in a very supplicatory position — there's lots of us around (especially saxophone players, we're two a penny), and it's highly competitive. The Musicians' Union has helped to fix rates in places where we would other-wise sell ourselves short and so be prised apart. Musicians are their own worst enemies, for example on occasions they may go and play in venues for next to nothing, and so bring down the rates for anyone following. Many of these people aren't professional which is fine — but finally everyone suffers, including those of us who are trying to earn a living. If people actually offer to play somewhere for almost nothing, then there's nothing that the MU can do about it. They can't do much for musicians with an individual grouse either, if you have one, you have to sort it out yourself through the small claims court. The MU don't really like being dragged into arguments, but they will help out as much as they can wherever possible.

If you study and practise properly, your instrument

almost plays itself. I've kept my ears open, done what my different teachers have told me, accepted styles, experimented a lot and I'm always ready to try new things musically. I feel I've paid all my dues now. I can't say for sure that I'll always be earning my living as a musician, if this life doesn't work for me, I won't go back to playing in dance bands etc, I'd rather go and do a daytime job that I could do with more sincerity.

The Other Musician

There are a wealth of musicians who earn their living by concentrating on their own individual skill and craft rather than marketing themselves on vinyl as a 'pop' product. They may be classically trained, all have a training of some sort, as they are required in their jobs to rehearse professionally, using sight-reading skills to a high standard. Most of these musicians are freelance, and they may be heard one week playing the saxophone break on a record, or the next backing a jingle for a radio commercial. Turn on the radio or television and you'll hear most of the jingles, incidental music etc made by these players, using their diverse skills to play classical, jazz or pop.

There is a whole living to be earned which is nothing directly to do with the Top Twenty: West End Shows, cabaret, advertising jingles, film music, radio sessions, pop 'sessions' live or recorded. Usually the repertoire of the freelance musician will include a good proportion of the Top Twenty tunes, although they'll find themselves repeating the more popular tunes many times over the years. It's possible to do extremely well at this career, although, as with many other careers, you may find yourself working with many less successful — or more jaded — than yourself. Some may have spent the last 10 years as a Butlins Camp musician, and, perhaps understandably, now have little enthusiasm or musical creativity left within them. These are the stop-watch musicians, who play their instruments without rehearsal in between, and think more about the money they're receiving than the show they're backing. An annoying trait perhaps, but imagine playing the same notes night after night in some long-running West End musical. It should be stressed, however, that competition among good freelances is fierce, and a good personal reputation is essential, not to mention membership of the Musicians' Union.

Chapter 2
The Manager

Introduction

There are two kinds of manager. One is the hustler, shaking up his unknown band, lifting them from obscurity to a solid existence by means of trickery and clever marketing. The other is a businessman, handling the monetary affairs of his hit act, making sure they maintain a good image in the public eye, making sure they don't pay too much tax, and acting as a buffer between them and the cruel world so that their creative souls remain fruitful.

Most people get into management through local bands that they represent, in the beginning out of friendship. Further up the ladder is the professional manager who goes out and talent scouts, almost like the record company a & r man. He, too, has a service he can offer a band, if only through his experience and contacts within the industry. At the lower end of the scale, however, the manager is necessary only for his personality and his faith in the act he represents. It's always easier, so the philosophy goes, for a supposed stranger to go to a record company or an agency and say 'Look, I know a band who you must sign immediately — I think they're great', than for the band themselves wandering around, perhaps slightly unsure of themselves to say, 'Please sign us, we're great — we think'. The fact that you've got at least one fan to speak up for you shows that someone has confidence in you. At this level, the manager is as useful as a fifth member of a four-piece band — he's eating, drinking and living the band's music, without him they would fail. So he's entitled to a fifth share of any proceeds of the deals he negotiates.

Once the band have been approached by a professional manager, however, the share-out is slightly different, according to how much they think he can do for them. A professional manager isn't going to become involved in the love-life of the lead singer, or in replacing guitar strings at three o'clock in the morning. His job definition doesn't include those duties, quite properly. He's there to hype a band up as many rungs of the ladder of fame and fortune as he possibly can, working in a creative marketing capacity, trying to expose the act to as many people as he possibly can. Whether or not they have what it takes when he's put them there is entirely another matter — it's up to them to produce the right quality records and play the right live set which the public can appreciate and enjoy. No manager can claim to have hyped a band all the way to the top of the ladder — he can only hype them as far as the stage or studio door, after that, he has to cross his fingers and pray.

So what are the first duties of any manager, after he's approached the band and convinced them that he can do a wonderful job, better perhaps than the person they have looking after them at the time. Should he wave a water-tight contract in front of them, guaranteeing him 15 per cent of their income for the next 20 years? He would be wasting his time if he did — there's a saying in the music business that there isn't a contract made that you can't drive a steamroller through, should the urge take you. It's true that if an act suddenly starts to hit the big time it's wise to organise something which will guarantee you at least a decent pay-off should a split occur, but it's also true that if you and your act have ceased to communicate fruitfully (that is, you hate the sight of each other) then heaven and hell can't keep you together.

Back to the first move. The manager and band sit round a table together and decide exactly what they want out of each other. It may be at this stage that they discover a total inability to communicate — the prospective manager may have a pop career in mind whereas the band members are happy to remain in the jazz clubs. If this is the case, all concerned should shake hands and go their separate ways. If the chemistry works, however, the band may be able to verbalise the next stage in their ambitions, which may be a few gigs, a publishing deal, a record on the steeets, or even a record on the streets which sells this time. The beginnings of a marketing plan should begin to be organised.

Investment

Should the manager invest his own money? Highly ill-advised, bearing in mind the unlikelihood of his receiving the money back. If the band are that good, it's better to leave it up to the publishing or record company to do the investigating. Money may have to be spent for example on telephone bills, while you are hustling the first few gigs for a good enough fee which can then be used as 'investment' money on: new equipment, an old van, tapes (forget something as good as a demo unless you're planning to turn it into plastic) and press-quality photos. Most of the initial invest-ment is time, which is more valuable to some than others — an enthusiastic manager may waste up to a year of his life hustling for a band which eventually split up and leave him — the loss is incalculable in terms of the opportunities he may have passed up in the duration.

Tactics

Step two for the manager is to get out and generate as much excitement around his act as possible, which is where the marketing talent comes in. Some bands are easy — they sell themselves into the Sunday papers through their eccentric behaviour. Others are a little harder to sell, but if the talent's there, it shouldn't be too hard to push it past the barriers. The marketing man of the century so far is Malcolm McLaren, who launched the Sex Pistols onto an unsuspecting public back in the mid-seventies, with all the punk explosion that happened immediately after. The Pistols were his creation, his baby — he conceived the idea, moulded it into shape through some carefully-planned anti-publicity publicity stunts, and the world watched in wonder.

His talent now is being directed towards BowWowWow, whose young lady lead singer is never far from the public eye. Of course he's had some horses along the way, who, once at the water, couldn't bring themselves to drink, but Malcolm's persistence will keep him in the business for a long time to come.

Most managers, of course, don't lead their artists quite as publicly as Malcolm, who relies a great deal on his own charismatic personality and 'star qualities' to sell his acts. In the majority of cases it's the star qualities of the act itself which can be exploited by the clever manager.

One of the best showcases around is the public appearance, which has to be arranged in the first place by the manager, who then telephones everybody possible about the show — or shows, making each call a little different depending upon whom he's calling. A few days later the recipients of his attention receive something interesting through the post — a tape, a picture or a biography. If he's done his job well enough, there should be at least a few people along to his first showcase gigs. His time is spent being friendly — not pushy — as most people like to make up their own mind about an act in their own time. If he's new to the game, this is his first chance to make friends with the people he may be working alongside for the foreseeable future. If he's made a fool of himself by being over-pushy and the band don't have what it takes on the night, then it's his judgement which is held in doubt afterwards — effectively, he's just blown his career as a manager. Just think, the next time he begins to hype an act — it may be five times better than the first one he worked with — he's not going to be very credible.

Making friends and then keeping them (including the musicians he's working with) is the slogan of a good manager. You never know when you may need someone again, even if they've crossed you this time around.

Record Deals

The ultimate aim and object of the exercise for most artists is to have a bit of plastic they can call their own, and here there may be several courses of action. Fortunately these days there are two totally different methods with regard to record deals, and which one you push your act into depends entirely on that act. Some acts actually need enormous amounts of investment to get anywhere: a top record producer, expensive recording costs, fabulous videos to promote their singles on television and general high-fashion appeal. These acts have to aim themselves towards a major record company — no one else can help them. Their market is basically affluent, people who listen half-heartedly to Radio One and wait for something stunning to leap out at them through the general dross of the day. They can afford to go out and buy videos, and their record shop is to be found at the back of one of the major chainstores on the High Street. They won't travel further because the rest of their time is taken up with following clothes' fashion. A band aimed at this market would die a death in an independent record company whose product is aimed at the motivated record buyer who is willing to spend time travelling to an indie distributor, or buying through mail-order. This punter will tune in to radio shows on obscure channels at unholy hours of the day and night to hear his favourite band. This sort of band doesn't need the investment of the major company to put across their music, which may be a form of pure aggression, excitement, political ideology or a mixture of all three. As regards marketing, all that band needs is column inches and airplay — their fans can be counted upon to seek out and buy their records.

If neither the major record company nor the local independent companies can be persuaded to put out product on your act even if you've presented them with a finished demo in a carefully put-together presentation pack, then it's not too much further to go to have a few hundred records pressed up yourself by your local pressing plant. It's the ultimate promotional aid, you can send it out to radio stations with sympathetic djs, to music papers and yet again to the record companies, who may finally be convinced that your act exists as a serious entity. You may even be able to recoup your investment by selling records at live shows.

After Signing

Assuming the band are finally signed to a record company somewhere, then, is the job of the manager really over? In fact, it's barely begun. Too many acts have banked their advances on a deal which requires them to produce an album a year for the next five years, only to find themselves back on the scrap-heap after the first duff record, put together in a haze of non-creative euphoria. The job of the manager is to keep the band alive, creating interest for them when they can't do it for themselves, off-stage or in the studio. In a major company a newly-signed act may find that some of its profits are being used to offset the losses of another act, instead of, more justly, being used to further promote that act. If your act wants special treatment from the company, then the manager has to be seen to be performing better than the company, showing them to be lagging behind in their press and promotions.

If he's out there in the market, hustling up press and promotions, then he's in a much stronger position to demand proper marketing investment when the first album is released, or the second single, say. The record company would be unable to excuse themselves with 'Sorry, we don't think there's enough happening on the act to warrant our expenditure here'. By definition, the record company and the manager always have to be diametrically opposed — although the ultimate aim is to get records out and sell them. The record company must represent the interests of their sales figures, whereas the manager is still in there, representing the interests of his artists so that they don't become swallowed up by the label, and so that he always has a say in their direction.

If your act makes it big, start hiring the best tax accountants you can find and set up as many tangible companies as are feasible. A good manager keeps the pot boiling, doesn't allow his artist to be overexposed, overworked or overworried, and he doesn't keep his eggs in any one basket for too long. But advice for managers at this level is fairly irrelevant — if they've got there, they must, by definition, know how to advise themselves.

Case Study

Bill Gilliam is one of the many agents — turned manager around who have seen the music business from both sides. When he left school he began managing a gang of musician friends because, he says, he didn't have a driving licence. If he'd had one, he would have been appointed their official roadie, and his story might have been different. He tried to join them, buying a saxophone and taking music lessons, but his lungs weren't up to it, and he went through reed after reed in his ham-fisted efforts to play. He bought his new reeds from a well-known music shop, where he became friendly with the assistant behind the counter — Paul Kossof. Paul persuaded Bill to come and take a look at his unknown band, called Black Cat Bones which, on seeing, Bill realised were light years ahead of his school-friends. He started managing Black Cat Bones with enthusiasm and obtained a record deal for them and lots of live work. After a while he joined an agency himself, taking his band with him, and for the princely sum of £13 per week, launched himself into a career as an agent. By this time he had the music business 'bug', and decided to make it his career, for love rather than money. He now has extensive management interests, an independent record label, and, although he has all but abandoned his agency work, he can still manage to organise the occasional live date should the need arise.

> As far as I was concerned then, working in the music business was better than working for a living! I would doubt that sentiment now, although I'm involved in the most rewarding part of the music Industry. I would never have been able to work in a major record company I always knew that the free-dom of management was infinitely preferable to that kind of job, and now that I am releasing my own records as well, I think I'm in a very good position at last. Management has changed since my early days with Black Cat Bones, whom I

was pleased to see evolve into Free, although the principles are basically the same — creating and keeping alive an interest in an act.

When I first went into management I thought I was going to make a vast fortune. I thought that all my dreams and aspirations would come true. After about five minutes I discovered that that wasn't going to happen without enormous amounts of hard work and luck. But I didn't want to go and be something else — I knew I wanted to stay in the business, maybe working with acts who have only got a few rungs up the success ladder — I find it satisfying to take them even that far. Most people who join bands are happy to at least have had a fair try, all they ask is the opportunity to be presented to the public in the way they want. It's the manager's job to put them onto the pedestal where they can say, 'Look at me.' to all who want to listen. Of course, if no one wants to listen, there's nothing you can do about it. My philosophy with a band, which has always paid off for me, is to be totally open and honest with them. If I feel that there's nothing more I can do for them, I tell them frankly. I can't stand the attitude of many people in the industry who avoid issues by not returning phone calls, or promising to do things without any intention of carrying them out. The next thing they know, a band is gossiping about them unfavourably in some bar, maybe to someone they're about to do a deal with. You have to remember that the music scene is tiny and very close. When you're a manager, you rest on your reputation, so it's important to stay friends with people even when you can't do business with them any more.

I've thrown my lot in with the independent scene now, after many years of cynical dealings with the majors. They set up departments with 'talent scouts' in them, but there is then such a net around them that it's almost impossible to get through. The situation is that the few bands who do get through are the ones who get signed. I've come across executives who say, 'I think this band are great, I think they'll go a long way, and when it comes to the Tuesday meeting I'll certainly vote with the majority . . .' What it boils down to, is that they're not so much interested in selling hundreds and thousands of records, as they are in keeping their jobs. When I've had an act signed to a major, I've taken care to keep every department in the company on the boil; I never called them unless I had good news, and I certainly didn't visit them unless I had something really exciting and new to put in front of them. You have to bear in mind that they're only human — they get as bored with their jobs as the next man — and they need as much of a sales job by the manager as does the public, or the whole thing stagnates. I think we are in a situation now where most of the majors now know exactly where their market is, their a & r department is almost redundant — they've been replaced by the independent record companies, who by the very nature of their existence have their finger on the pulse.

The biggest mistake a manager can make is to try and thrust his own ideas on an unwilling band who just don't want to know — that's when you go badly wrong. A good manager is someone who represents the interests of the artists in the way they want to be represented; if they've got what it takes and you've marketed it properly, then it will all come through.

Chapter 3
The Agent

Introduction

Agency work is something you're either born to or not, although everyone who wants to work in the music business would be well advised to spend at least a year in an agency somewhere. It's one of the best and possibly the hardest, training grounds as well as being the clearest vantage point from which to see the industry and decide which facet of it suits your own personality. An agent is there to look after all the live interests of an artist, which basically means he's something of a whipping boy for the rest of the record industry.

For the larger acts, touring is no longer a sensible financial proposition, particularly as less and less people are prepared to spend their hard-earned money on a one-hour show, when they could just as easily — and much more comfortably — be sitting at home watching their favourite act on video, or, listening to the record. From the record company point of view, there is no tangible evidence whatsoever that live work sells any extra products, so they aren't too inclined to pour vast sums of money into what seems to them an extravagant luxury. The largest indoor venue in this country is the National Exhibition Centre in Birmingham, which holds just 10,000 people — the size of a medium-range American venue. (This also explains why it's so hard to persuade a major US act to take time out to tour over here for any reason other than prestige, in world terms the UK market is so tiny as to be insignificant for most major acts.)

Bearing in mind average ticket prices these days — you

may still be paying off the mortgage on the last festival ticket you bought — it certainly sounds as if there's money to be made in live work. But a closer look at the workings of even a medium-range concert over here shows that to be a fallacy. On a purely basic level, there are hotel bills to be paid, vans or trucks to be rented (with experienced crew to drive them), and sound and lighting equipment to be rented (with experienced crew to set them up and work them). In addition, there are stages to be built, scaffolding, stage scenery (which gets more and more outlandish as the years go by — major acts know that their audiences expect something a little more to their shows than just good music), halls to be hired (most halls take a percentage of the door money these days), security men to be hired, as well as a very good tour manager to put all the bits together on the night and smooth over all the myriad problems that occur with a band on the road. That's the show itself.

Also out of the ticket money will come the cost of posters, advertising and all other kinds of advance promotion, as well as huge telephone bills for all concerned, and staff and office overheads. So it's not surprising to learn that most tours end up in deficit — a loss which must be covered by record royalties. The hope is that the amount of press received surrounding the tour has sold enough albums to make the whole charabang worth the effort. Most bands tour purely to promote some kind of vinyl product, rather than for love of Hilton Hotel breakfasts or endless hours of boredom on the M1. Nowadays they're far better off financially if they stay at home and produce an expensive video of themselves. This is potentially going to be seen by more record buyers than if the band spend an exhausting two or three months on the road playing to 80 per cent houses.

So why does the agent bother? After all, he's only receiving 10 to 15 per cent of the income, hardly enough to make it worth his while, one might assume. That's so true with rock acts that at the last count there were only a dozen or so companies left handling agency work and most of those have now diversified into management or promotion to bolster up their bank balances. Between them they represent most of the major acts you can think of, that still work live. Some giant acts of course don't need agents to look after their affairs, they can go directly to a major promoter and leave it to him to promote a couple of Wembley Arenas each year. But those who also like to tour Europe extensively and make their live appearances more than just a token gesture to the fans really need an agent.

He is a specialist. He knows through experience every promoter in Europe, as well as a good few around the rest of the world. Many agents now spend half the year in countries such as Japan, Australia and America with their British acts, smoothing over the culture shock, dealing directly with the foreign promoters, and setting up deals for the future. Unlike the totally insular attitude of more foreign agents, our British men are to be constantly found propping up bars in the major cities of the world, spreading the word about their acts; it is mainly due to them that British music is still the most highly regarded in the world.

Obviously most agents still have acts on their rosters which need to be sold as hard as possible at a lower level — the act who's maybe had just one or two minor chart hits, and for whom a live tour is a vital part of the career-building process. Then it's just a question of telephoning as many potential promoters as possible (here the college circuit can play a major part — its role on the live circuit varies from year to year according to the enthusiasm of the residing social secretaries) and the smaller clubs in the major cities where it's hoped the music journalists will be found lurking, notebook at the ready. These so-called 'happening' acts don't have to wait long before they're approached by an agent, who may offer anything from a three-month trial period to a firm agency deal which may run for several years. The offer will vary according to just how much the act is 'in demand'.

At a lower level still, there are myriad acts who desperately need to work live in order to survive, but who don't know how to go about finding work. They know, for example, that the best way to chat up an a & r man from a record company is after a good London gig — and, indeed, there are few agents who will take on a fairly unknown act without having at least seen it perform live once. So there's a fair amount of 'self-starting' which has to go on. An act will have to be prepared to book itself into venues by approaching the promoter or club manager direct until it gets to a level where a professional agent will even consider it.

The agency business, as has been stated already, is tiny. Most agents and 'bookers' are ex-college social secretaries — that is to say they've been running social events at their college before coming into the professional world. The advantage of entering the agency business this way is that you have a year or so to prove your worth over the tele- phone, and in how you run your events. If you show your- self to be enthusiastic, friendly, efficient and above all to have a good business sense, ie your promotions succeed, then it's fairly obvious that you are a saleable commodity.

Some agents have been taken on through other avenues, for example, they may have been booking out their own small acts from home for some time, or running their own small agency office for homeless acts, too small for the majors to notice. Those people soon discovered that agen- cies for small acts — those going out regularly for less than £500 per night, say — had absolutely no chance of making any money. Without exception, over the last ten years, every small-time agency has failed financially, and the best booking talent from those offices has been absorbed into the larger operations. So running your own agency from home for a few local acts if you're really desperate to enter the agency business that way, may not be such a mad idea. (Note that professional agents must be licensed by their local authority.) If you can make it even partially work, book your acts into venues for break-even fees, organise contracts efficiently and without too many huge mistakes, then undoubtedly someone somewhere will need your services in their company at the end of the day. Keep your most happening acts close to your bosom, there's no agent quite so in demand as the one who can bring a few hit acts into the office with him, potential income included.

From Agency to where?

There are some people who started life as agents before any of us were born, who will die agents long after us and take 10 per cent from St Paul at the Golden Gates just for the pleasure of their company (or more likely 15 per cent from Beelzebub at the other entrance). For those people there's an enormous pleasure in 'discovering' a relatively unknown act, planning its career alongside the management, helping to find the record deal (even negotiating it in some cases), and then slowly building the career over a number of years until they're eventually taking 10 per cent for Wembley appearances without even picking up a telephone to earn it. For them, agency life isn't just cold economics, it's a series of 'I remember the good old days' stories about booking Genesis into their local college for £50, etc. The cabaret world, in particular, is full of these wonderful gentlemen, who have reached the pinnacle of their careers and can now settle back in their swivel chairs while the Morecambe and Wises of this world earn them their cigars. They can book your grandmother into a rock and roll club from a broken-down telephone box — they'll manage somehow.

For the younger breed of booker, however, who spends his early days in the business being the middle man between the record company, the manager and the promoter, agency life must offer something else. And naturally enough it does, remember the agent is usually the first on the scene when an act starts to take off; he is in an ideal position to vye for management positions. Many of the managers of our most major acts were once the agent. Not enough agents go into a & r positions in record companies — the reason given for this is that just a short time within an agency demonstrates the inefficiency of the major record companies. They spend a fair amount of time, so agents complain, battling with record companies whom they say are 'too short-sighted' to appreciate the career boost that live work gives to a signed act. Many other agents go straight into professional promoting, after a few years of working alongside promoters, they learn how to do it themselves — and more importantly — build up the necessary professional contacts to make promoting a serious venture for them. As with nearly everything else in this business, the success of your career depends more on *who* you know, than *what* you know.

Case Study

Nigel Morton is 29 years old, and one of the few agents who came into the business without having been a college social secretary. This makes him a rare but perhaps slightly tougher breed of agent, whose hard business sense has been shaped through personal economic necessity; this contrasts with the slightly more academic approach of many of his contemporaries. His main qualification for entry into an agency office was a mania for music — he claims to have followed the Who to every British date they ever played during his youth. This was translated into the enthusiastic management of a local act, for whom he negotiated a respectable record deal, as well as a deal with the agent who eventually became his first employer. Unfortunately the office he moved into was a 'small' one, with too few money earning acts to pay the telephone bills. It soon folded, leaving him with no money but by now enough confidence in his own ability to set up his own company, backed by an 'outsider'. He, unfortunately, decided, after some time, to close what by then looked like a successful operation — though never successful enough for an outside investor. By this time, however, Nigel had established himself with enough of a personal reputation as an agent to warrant being taken on by one of the major companies. He is now a director of one of London's top agencies, with about half a dozen of his own personal acts and extensive connections throughout Europe and the States.

My mother blames it all on Dave Dee, Dozy, Beaky, Mick & Titch, if you can remember back that far! She says after I heard one of their singles as a child I changed completely —

and I've been going downhill ever since − personally I think I've got where I am now by never being afraid to say I could do something better than anyone else. Once you've convinced others that you're serious, there's nothing left to do but go ahead and prove it.

In the early days I realise I was very naive, but enormous amounts of energy and enthusiasm made up for it, somehow. Obviously I feel that any agent must be endowed with a certain amount of intelligence − you have to be able to think on your feet and be able to work out a good deal for a band − there's no one else who'll do that for you. You must have a good idea of where you're going and what you are going to do with the overall careers of your acts. Most agents are ex-college social secretaries, which does give them an added advantage − they've had a year at least of apprenticeship, running events at someone else's expense. They can also meander their way through the minefield of Student Union rules which are thrown at you in varying ways when you're booking acts into colleges − such as who in the Union has the authority to sign contracts, etc. These days I realise that most of all that is irrelevant, and I can ignore it, but it can be a major stumbling block for a novice.

I'm glad that I tried lots of different things since leaving school, there was a time when I thought I'd never find a career that I could contemplate remaining in for the rest of my days. Now I realise that I don't see myself as being able to do anything else except within the entertainment industry. I might extend into cabaret as I get older, it's much safer than the rock circuit from the point of view of agency work, as cabaret agency is so well established with traditions which go back so many years. It would be hard for a cabaret act to rip off his agent, for example, something which happens too frequently at our end of the business. On the other hand, I like to involve myself totally with my acts from the word go. It's true to say that if you can't establish the trust and confidence of a band, then it's not worth booking even one date for them.

An unknown act can be worked easily in their own area, or in the smaller venues in London. I try hard to have my acts seen by music journalists as I think that's a vital part of building an act both here and abroad − it's incredible just how closely read our music press is around the world. Obviously it's much easier to sell an act which has had even a review in one of the weeklies. I do take on unknown acts, but I am one of the few agents left who is prepared to. Unfortunately it's the case that it's much easier to book an act − and to promote it − when there's some product out, and the backing of a record company with all that that entails. There's just too much at stake to risk taking on too many completely untried acts.

Agents always work three months ahead of themselves at least — it may take even longer to get a return on your initial investment. And phone bills are horrendous — really. In this office there are just three of us — another senior agent as well as myself, and a junior booker (ex-social secretary) who looks after the colleges. I'll put together the skeleton of a tour for one of my acts, and the flesh will be put in by my colleagues. We sit down with the manager of the band and work out just where he wants his act to play, and when. As far as Europe is concerned, product and tour support is absolutely vital or they just won't be interested — Europe is very cost restrictive as far as that sort of thing goes. We are very lucky in this office — we handle a lot of acts who are good at promoting themselves without any help from record companies or us, which all makes our job very easy. Some of our acts are beginning to break the west coast of the States single-handedly, which is very exciting.

I have a small daughter now, so I don't want to do the amount of travelling that I once was expected to. I still have to go out about three nights a week, though. Fortunately I have an understanding wife! I suppose the main perk of this job is that you can go to any venue you like without paying, and meet people who, if you are a music fan, are important to you. You've got to be a music fan to do this job — you'd soon be seen through by the others if you weren't — and you would tire of listening to many different kinds of music after a few months, let alone a lifetime.

Chapter 4
The Record Company

Introduction

The British record industry is going through a revolution. In their youth, major companies comprised a coming together of bright, enthusiastic young men who created a need for themselves and shaped the public taste in music by promoting artists such as Buddy Holly and Chubby Checker. They brought music into the leisure time of the working public, instead of to a chosen few. The charts then were an excellent cross section of what the public actually wanted to hear and was buying. Now those same record company men are 30 or more years older and their enthusiasm for music has vanished. In its place is more likely to be a passion for racehorses or South Sea islands. Also in its place is a hard-nosed, cynical knowledge of how to sell records, regardless of their worth or display of talent.

The last few years have actually seen an increase in the number of 'man-made' bands in the charts. The recipe is as follows: take one song from a reputable team of writers, a good-looking girl or girls, a finished record and an appearance on Top of the Pops, result — one hit single, more to follow. Of course this kind of chart cookery assures a nice living for everyone involved, but the public are being duped and the backlash has already begun. It has started where it always does, among the real youth population who always have, and always will, know what they want — though not necessarily how to obtain it.

This chapter will outline both the workings of a major company, and those of a good, successful independent company. The first you may wish to join and work for. The second has no room for you, but may inspire you to copy it and start up your own company, assuming that you have at your fingertips the 'talent of tomorrow' to unleash on an unsuspecting public.

The Major

The first contact that a band has with a major record company will be via the a & r department. This stands for 'artists and repertoire', a term which hasn't been used for years, but which derives from the old principle of the a & r man who actually used to choose the songs for the artist to record. This still happens to a certain extent today in the case of artists who are essentially interpretive in their approach, and must therefore rely upon contributions from good songwriters to record (Cliff Richard is a good example of an interpretive artist).

Most a & r departments are small — a two- or three-man team. They are constantly out scouting for acts on the live circuit, listening to tapes, talking to previous managers that they've dealt with about new acts, or even trying to poach artists from another label, if they feel they can have more success with them than has previously been the case. It is the responsibility of the a & r men to decide the length of an artist's contract and to negotiate re-signing him when his old contract expires.

When it is known that an artist is going to be signed to the company, then, the well-oiled cogs making up the rest of the operation move into action. Tapes are passed from the a & r department on to the press and promotions offices, and then to the label manager who works closely with the marketing department. He may work in a team of two or three, depending on the size and range of the label.

Most of the record company will turn out in force to the next live showing by the artist, to familiarise themselves with the product they are about to try and sell, as well as to generate enthusiasm for something which they may so far have heard only on a rusty tape! The press office will be there in force, taking a close look at the act's image and the kind of fans it attracts, so that they know in which direction to aim press interest and can achieve the best possible exposure for the artist. This doesn't necessarily mean blanket indiscriminate coverage, which could have a reverse effect, destroying any credibility the artist may have. The wise press officer chooses his press coverage carefully (assuming that there's interest in the first place — and it's his or her job to create that interest via good photo sessions or a creative 'angle' aimed at a particular paper).

The Press Officer

It's worth noting, that although some press officers have worked their way up through the record company from being secretaries, post boys or even office messengers, most have in fact been culled from either music trade papers or the music pages of the nationals, so that as ex-journalists themselves they are ideally placed to know the requirements of specific papers. To an outsider, the 'pop' journals may all look the same, but an experienced press officer will always know which journalist on each paper will actively *dis*like one of his records. This is an insight gained from hours of socialising on buses, in trains and nightclubs, with an expense account which must be justified at the end of each month in terms of column inches gained.

A word should be spared here for independent press people, often ex-record company officers who have left the fray to set up on their own and, in theory, only work with the artists of their choice. There are some well-known independent press officers around who look after the media coverage of such notaries as Paul McCartney, the Rolling Stones, the Who, etc, but who can also be persuaded to promote the interests of less popular acts for a weekly consideration. The advantages of these people over a record company office, that may be struggling under the burden of a 100-strong roster of hit acts, are obvious, though of course much depends on the individual press officer. There are many record company press officers who complain bitterly that as soon as an artist begins to earn a good income, he employs an independent officer for added prestige. These days competition is so fierce for press officer jobs that there are many excellent people working within the major companies.

The Label Manager

The man in charge of the coordination of all the various teams within a record company is the label manager. He is the one who decides, along with the head of marketing, how much money is going to be spent on marketing a band — not just advertising, but record sleeves, and promotional aids such as posters, badges, t-shirts, cardboard displays for record shops, etc. He also has to make sure that the sales force are going to be able to take enough advance orders for an album to actually warrant the spending of the aforementioned money. After he has received the tapes from the a & r department and decided on a realistic release date for the product, he then 'presents' as much as he can about the band to his sales force so that they can go out to the record shops and work for as many advance orders as possible. When dealing with a single, he has to make sure that there's enough 'activity' as regards publicity going on around its release to make sure that it has as good a chance as possible for selling and charting. This also means a maximum amount of radio play, of course, and the importance which record companies place on radio airplay cannot be overstated. This is where the promotions department plays a part.

The Promotions Department

This department exists to obtain maximum exposure for the company's records. Radio One and television programmes such as Top of the Pops, are known to be the most effective way of selling records. Appearing on Top of the Pops can make the difference between a top ten hit and a number one, as any of the bands who have regular chart hits will readily admit. There is no one too proud to drop everything, or fly from anywhere in the world, to appear on this illustrious and longest-running of pop programmes. It's worth noting that both Top of the Pops and Radio One cover only singles — there is no significant album airplay in this country similar to the 'FM' radio stations in the States. Therefore, the most effective way to sell an album over here is to have a single connected with it in the charts. Many single releases are desgined more as promotional aids for albums — which have a larger profit potential — than as solo efforts.

Obviously it's sometimes worth putting out a single on its own, without any kind of album back-up in sight, if it has a special value of its own, for example a Eurovision winning song, or something so totally unusual that it stands out from all the others. A good example of this was Aneka's 'Japanese Boy', which was presented to a record company as a finished product, all that had to be done was to release it and do the work to obtain press coverage and airplay. The record was hugely successful and undoubtedly made a good profit for both record company and artist. This, however, is unusual. When a record company signs an artist, it may be committing itself to three or four mediocre single releases, all of which cost enormous amounts in terms of company energy and finance, and which because of the tiny profit margin on singles may actually lose the company vast sums of money. It's worth it to the company, however, because a single gains some airplay, helps to establish the artist, and when eventually an album is released, it may recoup everything.

The Declining Market

The record industry is incredibly wasteful. It is not at all like the manufacturing of one specific marketable item (baked beans!) which can be endlessly and creatively repromoted — the only problem there is keeping it in the shops and keeping the consumer interested in it. The problem most record companies face is that consumers aren't particularly interested in buying records any more. The record market is a constantly declining one, and it's increasingly difficult to make someone buy a record just because it's on a recognised label which has an established track record. Companies are out seeking more interesting records, or records that they know people will want to buy — which is why a & r departments carry the most power within a company. A good talent scout, with a proven 'nose' for success, can these days command his own salary, within reason. Although, as the industry is so small, and the amount of new blood coming in to the majors each year can be counted on the fingers of one hand, a good talent scout is better off heading his own independent company.

Summary of a Major Company

Managing director — oversees the general policy of the company and organises licensing and distribution deals.
Marketing manager and marketing department — usually includes two label managers.
A & R department — reports directly to the managing director.
Promotions department — usually two people to cover Radio One and television, and another for the other radio stations eg Capital, Luxembourg and Radio London and a couple of assistants who involve themselves with mail-outs to discos, etc.
The head of promotions — he may be based in London for just a few days each week, the rest of the week is spent in the regions, servicing all media outside London, he is helped by a permanently-based regional team.
Press office — about four people in a large company: three press officers who share the acts between them, and one assistant whose function is to disseminate whatever information they have about their artists among the printed media. It can be just as important as the promotions department, in terms of creating an act.
Production department — of varying size according to the limits of the company. It is responsible for making sure that

49

the records are manufactured up to standard, and for liaising with the factory.

Sales department — many companies share a sales force with each other, as well as having a small resident team who make sure that justice is done to their own releases. On the road constantly is a team of sales reps. They visit record shops, and try to gain as many advance orders as possible for albums whilst servicing singles sales — making sure that if a single is getting lots of airplay then all the shops they call on should have adequate stocks. This team also serves as an invaluable feedback channel from the public. Larger companies may also have their own financial and business affairs department, as well as an in-house art team.

All the operating directors of the various facets within the company meet once a month to discuss where the company is or should be going. Although the managing director has final veto, most record companies are actually very democratic — they rely for their financial success on the enthusiasm, hard work and initiative of every individual within the company. During the sixties there was room within all these companies for nail-buffing or coke-sniffing 'beautiful people', but nowadays unless you can justify your job in real financial terms there is just no room for you.

Case Study

Andy Murray is the label manager of a major record company and has been in the music industry for about six years. He was elected social secretary at Leeds Polytechnic while doing a degree in graphics. During his last six months at college, he came to London to do a project on the music industry and spent some time interviewing and projecting his own not inconsiderable personality on music industry personnel.

When he finished his degree, he took the path of many social secretaries before him and joined an agency office, starting at the bottom end. He soon discovered that selling small unknown acts to other social secretaries was not to his style, and he left there to work in a major record shop in the West End of London, and on to help launch another shop for the same company in Brighton. His design talent and energy were useful when he joined the small staff of a trade magazine for promoters, which gave him the opportunity yet again to speak to potential employers in the record industry. His efforts were soon rewarded with the offer of a job as press officer with a burgeoning independent company, he accepted, but was rarely seen out of the office for 18 months. He moved from there to a large record company as product manager, and has moved twice more as product manager within major companies.

I am the man who decides how much money is going to be spent on an act in a marketing capacity. Although a lot of people think that my only function is to decide whether or not a band receives a double page spread in the music papers each week, at the other end of the scale there's a great degree of co-ordination involved — on albums, for instance. I have to make sure that the sales force are going to be able to take enough orders in advance to warrant any money at all being spent, so almost as soon as we have worked out a release date I have to prepare a presentation to the sales force to raise their enthusiasm. Also, I am the artist liaison man, the buffer between the act and the record company. Artists know that they can ring me up at any time with a query or a problem, and can expect an answer. I will also liaise with a sleeve designer which might either be our in-house designer, or he might by mutual agreement with the band and the band's management, be an outside freelance.

My boss, the marketing manager, and I discuss a marketing plan around the first single and subsequently an album. This will be based on where we think the band is going — it's not a question of us saying, 'Well, we don't like Black Sabbath's heavy metal image, we don't think it should be so strong: let's put them in satin suits and place an orchestra behind them,' that's not the case at all. It's more a question of what we feel is the correct 'handle' on the artist — which is basically appreciating what they're all about and to whom their music is likely to appeal. It's our function to take an act's style and translate it into advertising (if it's needed), press approach and promotion — which is going to be completely different for each act.

This is the part of the job I really enjoy, as it's where the chance for creativity comes in. As regards some bands, for example, it's a waste of time to talk about glossy magazines and new photo sessions, I just make sure the sleeve is ready on time and that the sales force have had a chance to sell it up front for at least a fortnight. Then, to give fans the chance to go out and buy it, I make sure that it's advertised in papers that supporters of that band will read. Similarly, radio is very important, and I make sure that the promotions department have heard it and like it and can suggest ways of having it played. So my job is basically co-ordination with all the departments in the company as well as close links with all the acts. It's very hard work and there's certainly no glamour involved!

The Independent

The difference between a major record company and an independent is economic; majors are struggling to keep afloat, pay huge staff and office costs, by trying to turn over enough 'units of product' per annum to keep the bank manager happy. Majors exploit talent basically, for their own benefit, although there's no doubt that this moneyed circle benefits the artists who are signed as much as the companies. Major companies can afford to spend up to (as in one recent case) £100,000 on an act they really believe in — no independent could afford to do that. This may be to the detriment of some artists who actually need expensive videos and other promotional pushes to put them in front of the public eye.

The independent, on the other hand, is usually a handful of people who believe so absolutely in the music of one or two acts that they sell their shirts, mortgage their mothers' houses and camp out in telephone boxes for that cause. In the case of most 'small labels' it's actually the band them-selves who've pooled their savings to produce a single. The amount of sales needed then to make some return on their investment is about 3000 — not too hard to achieve in this day and age. A major record company must sell five or six times that amount to make it worth while at all. So natur-ally majors have to gear their a & r policy towards acts which they feel confident will appeal to the majority taste — eg what Peter Powell would play on his Radio One family show. They simply can't afford to put out a record by an unknown, yet worthy artist, whose anarchistic politics appeal only to a passionate few.

Catering for the Minority

Minority taste, however, should not be stifled, everyone knows that what may be esoteric now may just be next year's big thing. Just ask the a & r men who listen avidly every night to the John Peel Show — Radio One's only acknowledgement towards the independent scene. Obviously there are valid criticisms that can be levelled against the independent market. 'A licence to publish dross', is a common complaint from anyone who is forced to spend hours of his time listening to virgin tapes. One small Bristol record shop which is itself the home of an independent record company produced the following comment recently, 'Our shelves are stocked at times with the most unbelievable rubbish possible from unlikely bands on unlikely labels — but we would never dream of exercising any kind of censorship of our own, by refusing to sell records that we don't like for one reason or another. We believe that people should have a right to play, record or listen to the music they choose — it only annoys us that public taste is so totally directed by the mass media — good independent records just aren't heard, so they aren't bought'.

What is Involved in Making a Record

Obviously it's easy to make a record, if you have the necessary finance. First you go into a studio and record it — you can either produce it yourself (why not have a go) or hire someone with a good 'ear' for your music to produce it for you. The studio time will include the cost of an engineer — you can't act as your own engineer without the necessary knowledge. Sometimes this can be the most expensive part of record production — the kind of band who need two years in the studio to perfect their music, could find that the bills run a little high. But if you're prepared to go into a studio during 'dead' time (such as the middle of the night) and you are sufficiently well rehearsed, then you can keep the bills for this part of the operation fairly low. Then you have to cut a master (using professionals, preferably) and send your finished product off to a record plant along with an order for however many thousand copies you think you can sell. A sleeve has to be conceived and thought of — including artwork, if you want an eye-catching cover and there may be artwork costs for the record label. Distributing the final product can vary from a stand at your local venue on the night you play there, to a deal with a company like Rough Trade, who will take a percentage of the cover price in return for handling the distribution of your single or album.

Distribution

Distribution is actually the point at which most good independent companies stumble — they may have an excellent band, but fans in Dundee find they can't buy the record at their local shop. There's a limit to the number of times they'll go in and ask for it, especially if their local record shop happens to be Smiths or Woolworths, who do not stock records held by any of the independent distributors. So if you really want nationwide, or even world-wide distribution for your band, maybe you should consider going to one of the majors and standing in the queue with the other 8000 acts. It's worth noting, however, that you'll certainly jump a few places in that queue if you're holding on to your own independently produced single which has already seen some action of its own in the independent charts. This will prove that despite poor distribution, lack of your own promotions team complete with in-house plugger who plays golf with Radio One producers, you've still managed to create interest in your act. A worthy reference to throw in the face of the poor beleagured a & r man.

Investing in Other Acts

If your single has sold 3000 copies and you've actually made a few pence, you could decide to invest some money in another act whose music is worth your time and energy. By now you have a label called perhaps 'Rotting Fish Records'; there's no doubt that if the first single were a success, that would bring an enormous boost to the second single. Choosing an act in which to invest your own hard-earned money puts you in almost the same position as the a & r man, with a few notable differences. Firstly, your job doesn't depend on finding a huge money-making smash — luckily for you, because there's not many of those around. Secondly, you have the freedom to decide whether or not you actually want to make your second signing a financial gamble. You may be at liberty to produce a single just because it's good, or because it says something that you want to record.

The much maligned anarchist band, Crass, have done exactly this with the proceeds of their albums and singles. Many of the other releases on the Crass label have been highly unsaleable poems and experiments in music, which no one else in his right mind would have released. Crass have been able to do so because of the money earned from their albums and singles. By following this policy, Crass Records have kept themselves a truly independent label, and, despite their occasional lack of taste, most of us should thank them for keeping the spirit of the independent alive by releasing only what they like, rather than what they hope the masses will like. The masses have an absolute right to enjoy the music of the Brighouse and Rastrick Brass Band, but so do the minorities have a right to listen to the lyrics of Annie Anxiety or the saxophonic cavortings of Ted Milton.

Case Study

Mike Alway is 26 years old and has been in the music business for five years in one form or another. He started by playing in a band and went on to manage another, which he had seen play 12 or 13 times at his local venue. He approached them and offered his support and enthusiasm. The outcome was that he acted as that band's agent, manager and, as he puts it, their 'whipping boy' with a £600 telephone bill to pay after organising a nationwide tour for them singlehandedly. This followed a universally planned album release, and was a financial disaster.

He then turned his attention to promoting, and found a small-town pub venue. The management was prepared to let him experiment with alacrity, while it kept the bar profits. The venture was a huge success; mainly through his own good promoting sense and hard work, the venue became very popular. Soon, the idea was put forward to produce a compilation album of the best bands which regularly played the venue. Mike started to direct his energy towards possible record companies as backers. Eventually, one of the smaller independent companies admitted to him that it would have been delighted to work with at least eight of the twelve bands he had compiled for the album, but it didn't have the staff facilities, or the time. The company offered to take him on part-time to continue his project, and develop others. It wasn't long before Mike became the company's key man, handling a & r, press and promotions. He now has one assistant to help him with press and promotions which puts the total staff strength of the company up to five.

As far as I was concerned, it was just a question of wanting to do it enough which brought me to where I am now. I left school early without any qualifications, and actually worked in an insurance office for four years, but abandoned that literally over night for something to which I knew I could be totally committed. I was lucky at that time to be living with my parents, without any responsibilities, or that move would have been impossible, but I wanted to be in a position where I could have the freedom to be creative. Personally my biggest weakness is financial limitations — I find it very hard to see the practical side of the music business, therefore it's good working under a boss who has an accountant's mentality as far as that sort of thing goes. I hope that I'm learning from this, so that when I leave to run my own record company much later, I will have got rid of some of my old bad habits. Having said that, however, it seems to me that in order to enter the music business you just have to know the right people.

I find bands to sign from a variety of sources, from demo tapes to just keeping my ear to the ground — we seem to make a habit of signing bands that other labels have dropped. It's not a deliberate thing, but there were a mass of successful independent bands around a few years ago who were picked up by the majors and produced one or two records, and these weren't as huge as the majors had hoped, I think. Those bands are now available to us again — back where they should have been all along.

I tend not to go looking for bands live, because the live circuit in London has become far too condensed. I could go to 30 gigs in a row looking for a band to sign, but would be unlikely to find one. My time is better employed listening to records and tapes. There just isn't enough time in the day to cover both activities. Then if I'm definitely interested in someone, the first thing I do is to bring him into the office for discussions. Obviously how we get on at a personal level is very important — it doesn't always work. We'll look at a policy for the first year. Usually the band themselves will have a very definite idea about how they want to start off — a single, followed by an album. I liaise with my boss, who works out the deals to see if we can actually afford it. I like bands to sign on a long-term basis, obviously that's not possible with every case, but as a general rule I think it's a good idea to begin the relationship so that the band is thinking in terms of a long career with us.

All the jobs involved in releasing a record are kept as much as possible within the family, so to speak. All the people on this label are here because they want to be — we are absolutely committed to each other. After finding the band, signing them and bringing them into the studio, I usually cut the records myself. I then, helped these days by an assistant, handle press when it comes out. As far as promotion is concerned, I an not actually against the idea of advertising — it is, after all, a way of informing people who wouldn't otherwise know what we are doing. But when I look at the coverage which acts such as Rip Rig and Panic received for their first album, in terms of full-page adverts in all the music papers, I'm not so sure it's really what sells records — after all. Their first albums sold no more than 6-7000 copies, and were probably unlikely to have sold any more than that anyway, bearing in mind their popularity at that time. A small company like ours would have been only too pleased with sales figures like that.

I don't see our company expanding hugely, and I hope that we would never have to sell out creatively. I would like to see an ideal situation in a few years time where we have two or three acts which sell over 50,000 records each time they release something. Then I would like to have a few acts which always sell around the 15,000 mark, there would never need to be any commercial pressure put upon them to sell more. The remaining acts on the label would only sell a few thousand copies of each release. I would hope never to be in a position where I could only sign an act which I knew would automatically appeal to the masses, regardless of its musical worth. I am aware that other companies who can now be counted among the majors — such as Virgin Records — started out just like us a few years ago. They have had since to come to terms with the economic realities of servicing a huge act, while not pouring thousands away upon the smaller ones. I hope that I can learn from their mistakes while still keeping the same musical base upon which my company now rests — that is an entirely creative one.

Do-It-Yourself a Crass Way

If you have any interest at all in the current musical scene then you've at least heard of — or even seen — Crass, who from the original punk movement a few years ago have developed an exciting and passionate way of expression involving what at first glance seem to be all the established music industry trappings. They play live, release albums and singles (admittedly at half the price of normal product), they release records for other bands on their own label (Crass Records) and run a business which to all intents and purposes could be taken for any other small concern in the industry. But there's one basic difference which sets this particular group of idealists apart from all the others and thus makes them the purest record-producing group to examine in depth: they're not in it for the money. Money corrupts in any business (ie in a sense that most product is produced with profit in mind, rather than people, they only become involved in the calculations when they affect the profit) but its corrupting influence is never seen more strongly than in any area involving creativity. Thus the main body of the music business is geared totally towards the mass market, records are released only when they can be sure of selling a minimum 20,000 units, preferably more. Minority interest music such as reggae, folk, punk, psychadelia or even rubber band music just isn't considered.

If you're doing something really new and interesting, you'll find the major record companies sniffing briefly around your ankles, but unless they can be sure of converting your artistry into a mass marketable 'fad', a sniff is all you'll get from them. Meanwhile, it's the independent record company scene which has stepped in to act as saviour to the many diversities of current music, much to the chagrin of the majors. They have, in many ways, tried to erode the popularity of the independents which they see as a threat to their profit potential. They do this either by offering to license small labels (you may think you're buying a Red Flame record, but actually it's funded by and distributed by Phonogram Records, a palpable major), or by offering huge sums of money to the better artists on the independent labels, to entice them away completely. This is why many of the independent labels have been described as 'stepping stones' to the majors.

What does a creative band currently on an independent label lose by signing to a major company? In the short term it would appear that they only gain — perhaps a large advance sum of money. However, it's important to remember, as has been explained in Chapter 4, that the term 'advance' means just that; the record company will recoup it out of your royalties and the larger your initial advance, the less likely you are ever to *see* a royalty payment. In the long term, however, the band have lost everything with which they started out. After the honeymoon with the record company is over, they may realise just how one-sided their deal — which is likely to have been negotiated to run as long as five years — really is. If they insist rigourously on keeping their original creativity, possibly to the detriment of their popularity, they may find the record company refusing to 'pick up' their annual option, which leaves them back on the streets where they began. If they play the game the company's way, they may become pop stars without any of the original aims and ambitions which first so inspired them. They have 'sold out' in every sense of the word. A hit single may involve visits to hospitals in the company of photographers, autograph signing sessions in the record shops of 'key' chart-producing cities, balloon races, radio phone-in sessions on vegetarian cooking and whatever else the marketing department can think of.

You may think that's fine — if so, signing to a major record company poses no moral problems. You may, on the other hand, be the kind of musician who feels that music is a way of changing the hearts and minds of the public. You may be a poet or a philosopher with something to say. You may find it a problem tied to a company who nod enthusiastically to your latest single and say, 'Catchy, yeah, love the music — perhaps we could drop the lyrics and insert "la-la-la" so as not to upset the Radio One producers . . .'

Crass have such a moral dilemma. At least, to them, there is no dilemma because so far they have managed to circumvent the money-filled pot-holes which cover the music industry road. They don't actually see themselves as even on that road. They play music, sing lyrics, make records, go on tour, but there, they say, the comparison between themselves and most bands ends. Politically anarchist, they have all been involved as a creative group for something like the last 15 years. However, it was only when Johnny Rotten of the Sex Pistols said in 1975, 'If you want to make a record, go out and do it,' that they decided to put their message onto vinyl, rather than in book, newspaper or poetic form. Their first ever record was a financial disaster, as they admit to having been a little naive about the hidden 'extras' of records — such as VAT, etc.

According to Andy Napalmer, the lead singer, 'We ran up a local pressing plant and asked how much it cost to press 1000 singles. We divided the price they gave us by 1000 and that was the cover price of the single'! The thought was there, though, and Crass soon shot to fame on

the independent scene — fans appreciated their total
honesty and commitment to their belief that releasing a
record doesn't necessarily have to involve huge profits for
record companies. Soon, their releases were selling more
than many of the Top of the Pops records, although they
had no hope of ever realising establishment recognition for
their success. This was not because, as one may assume, of
their slightly unusual politics or even necessarily because
many of their records contain some rather strong language,
but because the BMRB chart alone — to which only the
major record companies have access — is accepted by the
BBC, etc.

If Crass, therefore, signed a licensing, distribution or
even a full record deal (and they've had plenty of offers)
with a major company, they'd soon be gracing the BMRB
chart with their feminist, pacifist, anti-nuclear messages,
and no doubt causing great headaches for the Radio One
producers. However, from the comparative security of their
homely country cottage, they have been able, without too
much difficulty, to resist the temptations of large advances,
etc and have continued to sell records at cost price — their
current single is available at just 45p. This gives them just
one penny profit to pay the electricity board and the local
greengrocer. They have also incorporated a carefully cal-
culated profit into their album in order to fund projects
for other needy bands. Some of those have had great
success on the Crass Record label, but still manage to sell
their albums for half the normal recommended retail price.

When we first began, all that we knew about releasing records
was that it was basically a rip-off. Not only that, but most of
the records out on the scene promote ideas which are wrong
— such as sexism. When we looked more closely, however, we
realised that it *was* possible to put out a record and do it
decently and honestly, without ripping fans off, and without
promoting false ideals. We have proved that record prices are
simply far too high.

Our records are the same quality as those released by the
'established' record industry — if not better — because we
actually go down to the pressing plant and handle all the
quality control ourselves. We believe that if someone is going
to pay out good money for one of our records, it shouldn't

be warped — it should be the best quality we can manage. What we don't provide, which must count for at least half the cost of a normal record, is enormous amounts of expensive promotion. We don't advertise or involve ourselves in any of the costly hype indulged in by other companies. We feel strongly that if you put out something exciting and demanding, then people are prepared to make the effort to find your record and come to your gigs.

So far, word of mouth has worked very well for us. It would be lovely to imagine our records freely available down every High Street, but the moral cost of that would be too high for us. We'd have to sign a distribution deal with one of the major companies that may be earning its living dealing in arms, and it would instantly double the price of our records for its own profits; we couldn't live with that.

Although Crass are in agreement that they would like more people to hear their poetry and philosophy (to Crass, anarchy means personal responsibility, which every thinking person must feel in his heart, although that same person must despondently accept the total vision as little more than a romantic fantasy), they are still undecided as to just how far they should go to take their message further. The fact that their record sales are healthy by any standard proves that there is a portion of the record-buying public who doesn't need to be persuaded by glossy advertising and promotional gimmicks into buying a particular product. However, Crass do sometimes wonder whether there are a few others around, who may benefit from listening to their product, but who won't take a bus and travel miles to visit their nearest independent record shop. A poster campaign would undoubtedly be a help, but would necessarily raise the price of their records to cover its costs. Crass, however, are rarely short of bright ideas.

Large outlays of money aren't always necessary to put your name in front of the public. A few years ago we had the opportunity to sell an anti-marriage flexi-disc to a magazine called *Loving* — (they thought it was a typical romantic song which supported their ideology of the traditional marriage, where, we think, the woman enslaves herself to the man at the cost to her womanhood and membership to humankind, it wasn't) — we doubt if they even listened to it before they put it on their front cover, wedding bells and all. Needless to

say, there was a huge outcry as soon as the game was discovered, and we earned outselves the title 'Band of Hate' by
the *News of the World*. As a marketing exercise, though, if
you like to call it that, it was a huge success. It only cost us
the price of the flexi-disc.

Obviously, that kind of opportunity isn't going to present
itself too often, but a little imagination and inventiveness
can go a long way. Album covers, for example, don't have to
be superbly printed — they can be xeroxed and folded by
willing helpers.

They do admit to having the ability and willingness to
work for very long hours for 'the common good' rather
than a union wage. This means that albums can be sleeved
and prepared for distribution at virtually no cost, something which would be impossible for a company with a
turnover of millions rather than thousands of records, but
which again illustrates the potential success and advantages
of the small, dedicated company.

Crass also illustrate the lack of necessity of signing to a
distributor. Although companies like Rough Trade, Recrea-
tional, etc (the independent distributors) do handle a good
percentage of their product, they also use third party
carriers, who work just like the Post Office, carrying
records in bulk — and charging by weight — to individual
shops around the country. These shops then deal direct
with the Crass business element, namely John Loder at
Exitstencil, who also admits to having learnt 'the hard way'
about producing records. He comments as follows.

Between us, we've shifted literally tens of tons of records by
hand in the past, and sometimes the creativity has been a little
overbalanced by the sheer mechanics of putting out a record
which involves so much work. But the passion which drives
our particular machine makes it look Mickey Mouse by
comparison — what makes our operation a success is the
passion and sheer desperation of the people running it. We're
not a business as such, although there is a business aspect to
what we do, in terms of keeping books, paying tax and so on.
We still do things which are unbusiness-like, however, the
profit side of the operation is simply a by-product. If we
decided to do something which would make no profit, or
even a project which was worth folding the company for,
then we wouldn't hesitate to do it. That's why you can't call
it a business.

Andy continues.

> This is our life, most musicians probably feel the same to begin with, but it always seems to get lost along the way. Life simply isn't a brand new Fender Amp — it's worth more than that, and musicians should consider carefully when they are offered an advance by a large record company which would cover that. People put their life on their amplifiers or their guitars, but they think that their life is only two weeks long — and so it breaks down. The amplifier or the new guitar becomes a symbol of the corruption of their ideals.
>
> At sixteen you're out on your own, you are coming to terms with how to live and how to survive. Maybe you've seen or heard something which inspires you, but trying to live with that inspiration can be incredibly difficult. We know that one of the reasons why we've survived for so long as we are is because the average age of the people in the band is much greater than in most bands. We've evolved together over a long time, and learnt the hard way about the amount of nastiness people can put you through on the outside. Regarding a record contract, you should always take it to someone you can trust to explain it to you before you make any decisions.

Crass aren't members of any of the establishment music industry bodies, like the PRS or the MCPS which are further sources of potential earnings. They feel, however, that money from these sources is not really theirs, but is more a product of a self-perpetuating system. The PRS, for example, collects money from the BBC every time a record is played and gives it, on a mathematically worked out basis, to their artiste members. People such as Paul McCartney and Tony Hatch, therefore, are probably the largest PRS money-earners. Crass don't particularly want to become a part of this circus. 'If the BBC want to give money to the PRS then that's their business,' they state. Although they admit that they can foresee a time when they might join: if one of the bands on their label particularly asks them to, or if one of their own songs starts picking up huge airplay. Anarchism allows, it seems, for a flexible approach.

Crass also approach their live work with a policy of avoiding the established venues and the established promoters, whom they feel take far too much money on the ticket price for personal profit. Major artists, they feel, also take far too much in payment for their work. They don't however, see themselves as 'entertainers' which many of the pop bands would gladly admit to. 'If you define entertainment as going to a gig and meeting friends and sharing a common experience with them, then yes, in that sense we entertain. But we don't offer a fantasy or anything remotely escapist. The imagery, words and the whole evening that we offer are potentially confronting — though not physically, we should add.'

Crass have had to come to terms with the potentially repressive presence of security men at their gigs — something they once vowed they would never allow. They had enormous problems with disruptive and violent elements in their audiences which were making live work almost impossible. Even now, with careful security, they are encountering problems with council and police bans, owing to a basic lack of understanding of their ideology by some of the local authorities. The band have still managed a recent successful tour, despite all this, including a storming date in Belfast with hardly any violent trouble at all.

We're not trying to change the music business in any way — in fact we're using it in a way it has always been used, as a 'protest' element, although we're going much further in our protest than ever before. In the past, record companies took on new forms of musical culture, but that's all finished now. They don't care if they sell records or bombs, just as long as both make a profit. We're using records as a form of expression, and trying to keep it decent. A record can be both enjoyable and constructive — we know that we've entered into a field which is basically corrupt, and that's why we're so careful about everything we do. Independent record companies started for the most part with very good ideals, putting music before profit. But many found that after they'd made their first record, which didn't sell very well, they had to accept offers of help from the majors in order to continue doing what they genuinely wanted to do. Very soon they found they'd been bought out. That hasn't happened to us so far, we've had offers, but we've been able to resist them because, without being arrogant, we *are* special.

We've never set out to create new standards within something that's already existing, but to reject the old ones. As it happens, through what we do, new standards have arrived — for example, our rejection of the 'star' dressing room syndrome, where stars hid themselves away, has caught on — many bands are now following suit, and aren't just getting up on stage to promote their own egos.

We certainly aren't saying that everyone should go out and live the same way and eat the same things we do. What we're saying is that people should *think* more about the standard ways that we've been told that we should do things, and then decide for themselves whether they actually want to continue living in the same way. If they realise that they *don't*, they should again decide for themselves the way they do want to live. That is a very broad way of putting it, we're not saying, 'Look, this is how we do it, you should do the same', it so happens that this is the way that works for us. Other people may find or have found their own way of putting out a record which is better for them, and which suits them better than our way.

What we do say, is that the most precious thing musicians have is their integrity — they should carefully work out from the start exactly what they want from their musical career. People don't see the record business as a moral arena, but that's exactly what it is.

Chapter 5
The Studio

Introduction

For many, the complexities of making a record are a complete mystery and are likely to remain so. We've all seen films of bands recording, crushed together in tiny sound-proof rooms, one hand on the headphones, the other tapping out time in an effort to keep up with the last over-dub. Above them, in an even smaller room, they are watched over by technicians and producers, who twiddle, push and slide the rows of knobs and buttons which seem to engulf them.

It's here that tomorrow's masterpiece may be produced, or tomorrow's failure. The combination of powerful, creative technology and musical creativity knows almost no boundaries. To many musicians this is almost too daunting a prospect to handle. The quiet atmosphere of the studio is oblivious to the world outside. A musician who steps for the first time, from a busy street into the still peace of the studio, inhabited by so many 'old hands' who have worked with all her favourite 'stars' may be forgiven for an initial nervousness. It takes a kind of gall to stand in the middle of an otherwise empty room and sing to yourself, aware that, instead of an adoring audience of fans to encourage you, there is only a poker-faced technician or producer, your most discerning critic and yet your sharpest.

Record producer, Mike Howlett wrote a feature in *ZigZag* magazine a few months ago on the subject of 'first-time' recording musicians, commenting that as a producer it's 'Easy to get him confused by criticising too soon . . .' He suggests, '. . . leave room for the player to loosen up and settle into the unfamiliar sound of the foldback (the sound you hear through your headphones), run through the track a few times — then call him a brainless half-wit and threaten to break his legs if he doesn't get it right . . .'

Many musicians take little more than ideas and feelings into the studio with them, leaving it to the creative surroundings to hatch them into something a little more tangible. Of course, with studio time available by the rather expensive hour, that kind of approach could work out a little dear. They might be better persuaded to work out their ideas in a slightly cheaper rehearsal room, taking the finished product to the studio to record as quickly as possible. Choosing the right studio out of the many that scatter the country may seem a daunting task at first — although in the beginning, it may be the cheapest adequately equipped studios that command the attention. Studios have a variety of services to offer — there may be superb equipment capable of laying 24 separate tracks down onto one tape (known as a 24-track studio, the *crème de la crème*), or there may be a quiet, country atmosphere, with board and lodging, where the musician may hide indefinitely to recuperate artistic feelings previously suppressed during long hours.

All studios are credited on the back of album covers, along with the names of the engineers who worked on the albums. Some bands may be in the position to try and ape the success of a record by booking the same studio and asking for the same engineer to help them.

The Producer

Finding the right producer is a slightly more difficult task. Well-known producers are in much the same position as film stars; they work when, where and for whom they like. Their reward is usually a percentage of the royalties, quite fairly, as a top-selling album may be, to a great extent, the result of the work of the producer.

In many cases he is the Einstein behind the work. A simple song may become a massive production piece, with full orchestra, brass section and male-voice choir, all parts written, arranged and rehearsed by the producer, who may then decide to make the whole charabang sound as if it comes from the bottom of a well. The person who publicly takes the bow for the finished product is naturally the artist, who may simply have been following the producer's directions. Of course, being a producer is by no means a secure job — you're as good as your last album — and although the rewards at the top are such that it's worth the heartache of the early days, it's no career for a pessimist.

There is no apprenticeship which precedes a person reaching the lofty heights of record producer, although as a general rule the best record producers have had in-studio training as tape operators and engineers. Others have been successful simply because they were in the right place at the right time, as often happens in the music industry. Some producers may manage a band, who trust them enough to allow them to oversee a first record, and then discover that their 'ears' are such that good production comes easily to them. Those producers rely totally at first on the ever-present experienced engineer to provide them with the sound they want to hear, and of course with enough patience and teaching to cover their myriad blunders. At this level a production job really isn't worth a royalty. It's more likely that the aspiring producer is donating his time and energy to the band for as little as they can afford, or as much as he can negotiate. Escaping from the syndrome of producing vinyl just for the fun of it on the backs of patient engineers and friendly musicians, however, is easier said than done. Reputation-building takes time and energy.

Another 'quickie' way into the production seat is simply to be a famous musician. If you're the lead singer of a hit act, or the known 'brains' behind a world-wide success-story musical troupe of some description, there are literally hundreds of new young bands who would like some of your success to rub off on them. You may have rubber ears, but for them to be able to sell their first single on the basis that you produced it, is equivalent to a hefty promotional boost, albeit that you'll be in a position to demand a consider-able royalty. It's likely, also, that unless you're very creative, their single will end up sounding just a little too familiarly like one of your own. Only the very exceptional musician has been able to turn his hand to production with any trace of single-minded aloofness from his own musical career, producing records which have an individual strength of quality unassociated with his own personality. Dave Edmunds and Nick Lowe are good examples of this latter kind of producer, running two quite separate careers side by side without cross-over — the musician and the producer. Dave Edmunds began producing many years ago as a 'name' musician, but has since managed to overcome this handicap, earning himself a reputation as a fine producer whose dedi-cation to music shines through all his work.

Going up the Hard Way

Studios are always on the look-out for inexhaustible people. The hours worked by studio staff are crazier even than those worked by junior doctors. For some reason best known to themselves, bands book studio time literally at a moment's notice and then come and work for 24-hour non-stop stretches, expecting studio staff to be on call and in charge of the controls throughout. The way to prove your worth in a studio is to begin as a poorly-paid 'tea-boy' (a term of fairly ancient untraceable origin which no longer has sexist connotations — girls have as much right to apply for tea-boy jobs as boys). The tea-boy is basically a 'gofer' (go for this, go for that), expected to be willing and cheer-ful at all times of the day and night, sharing the workload with probably only one other, so that the hours he will work each week will be long.

The pay is terrible; there is a basic wage for the first 40 hours worked, and then a little more for each hour worked overtime. The 40 hours worked, however, may have inclu-ded a couple of overnight stretches, so you really are expec-ted to behave as a superman/woman. If a band want a stick of fresh celery at three o'clock in the morning, you will be expected to go out in the pouring rain, if need be, to beg, borrow or steal it. Tea, coffee, cans of beer, packets of cigarettes — you must cheerfully provide them all, dropping whatever else you may be doing to 'jump' to the order of a technician, producer or musician.

Nobody knows why this rigorous initiation period must be endured before you actually start learning anything in a studio — possibly it's a foretaste, or toughening-up process for the life to come. Studios receive hundreds of letters each week from hopeful would-be tea-boys, and of those they take on very few last the course, so perhaps it's a good weeding ground. The basic idea, if you're keen from a career point of view to work in a studio, is to get in there. Once there, you're in a position to be 'in the right place at the right time'. An intelligent, interested, keen tea-boy will soon be rewarded with promotion — you can show them that you're worth it. Academic qualifications required from the tea-boy are basic. When sifting through the mound of letters they receive, studio managers would like to see some indication of intelligence — articulacy and ability to think logically, usually indicated by the acquisition of English and maths O levels.

If you have impressed by your letter of application, an interview may be forthcoming. Just because studios have an 'aura' of pop glamour, doesn't mean that studio mana-gers are going to be the least impressed by an outrageous sense of fashion — they're looking for a hard-working, capable, cheerful tea-boy-going-on-engineer, not someone concerned with his own appearance, who is likely to be upset if his clothes get dirty.

Are there Jobs for Girls?

It is much more difficult for girls to find studio work — studio managers don't feel that they are in the business of setting the world to rights as regards equality of the sexes and their attitude towards girl applicants is fairly cynical. They believe that (a) they can't take the long hours (an incorrect belief which has been disproved many times, although it is a still popularly-held myth), and (b) that they'll run off with the first bass guitarist who makes eyes at them — ie that girls don't go into studios with any kind of serious intent to learn the business.

If you're a girl keen to learn studio engineering, then you'll really have to do some convincing — it's likely, for example, that higher academic qualifications than your male colleagues will be necessary. Bear in mind, however, that whatever your intent initially, you'll still be the subject of much sexual harassment. The music business, sadly, being what it is, a tired musician, taking a quick break during a long session, is more likely than not to have a 'roving eye', and if you're the only 'talent' around, it will quickly alight on you. The first liaison, however, and you're fired — and you've destroyed a careful path, built before you by girls trying to prove to studios that they really are more than willing sex objects. If you want to meet musicians all day, but aren't interested in a career, go and work as a receptionist for a record company.

No one's keen to employ anyone who can't cut the pace on her own merits — the sixties and early seventies, about which so much has been written, were the time when the odd 'pretty face' was a positive asset around the office, productive or otherwise. Nowadays they don't really care what you look like, just as long as you can do the job better than anyone else. If your pretty face is your only asset, you'll earn more and get further in another industry.

The Tape Operator

The next step up from tea-boy, if you're still alive by then, is tape operator — sometimes known under the title assistant studio engineer. All the sounds in the studio — even if recorded one at a time and built up on a 'layer' basis — go through a huge mixing desk to get the sound right, on to an enormous tape machine with up to 24 different recording capabilities. The final 'master' tape produced is usually two inches wide and holds all 24 recorded tracks in separate bands. Thus a saxophone line laid down on one (or even two, via two microphones — track, can be easily rerecorded or remixed without harming the other tracks. The machine has up to 24 dials, and it's the job of the tape operator to keep a close eye on which one is recording at which time — he must take care to channel the bass guitar, for example, through its own separate track. If the wrong track is switched on, a perfect track recorded earlier may be wiped at a stroke, on the same principle as a simple tape recorder at home. Once the basics of the machine have been grasped, it's another long stint ahead of keeping your eyes straight ahead and your ears open.

Whereas a bright tea-boy may be promoted to tape operator within a year, it may take three or four years to move from tape operator to studio engineer, but it's during this time that the essential job is learnt and experience gained. The hours are the same, the pay better than that of a tea-boy but now at last you are in the control room, learning about microphone techniques, different mixing techniques, computer-controlled desks and even what it takes to be a good musician. When the engineer leaves his post for a few moments, he may trust you enough to say, 'Take over until I get back' — rather like an understudy. If he is sick one day, you may be able to persuade a busy studio that you know enough about what the band want that day to work with them alone, or, more pertinently, you may be able to persuade the band of your worth.

Most assistant engineers remain in the studio which trained them to become proper engineers — but with some of the more established studios this could literally mean waiting for someone to retire. As engineers grow older, they may move into recording classical and MOR (middle of the road) music, keeping their seats warm and well-filled. An aspiring engineer in one of these studios may do well to put loyalty aside and seek positions further afield. Another responsibility for the 'tape op' is care of the final tapes, which may be held in a library of their own elsewhere in the studio building. These tapes aren't the ones used to cut the record — that is taken from a specially produced 'stereo' tape — made by yet another complex machine with the capability of putting all the tracks from the master together on to a two-track ¼-inch tape producing the final 'stereo' sound from which the master disc can be cut.

The Engineer

The engineer is the man who breathes life into the inspiration of the musician and the producer. A poor band may not be able to afford a producer, in which case they leave their art in the hands of the studio engineer. He must be trusted to present their music in the best way possible, pulling everything he can from the many boxes of tricks at his command to create the product they want, preferably in the most relaxed way.

The studio engineer may have to work alongside — and under the command of a fairly inexperienced producer who may understand nothing of the technology which surrounds him. It's up to the engineer to help as tactfully as possible, translating the ideas of the producer — which may be good, if technologically inarticulate — to a workable reality which will please him.

The intricacies of the various microphone capabilities are something learnt through long experience — the good engineer knows how to get the best from the equipment around him. He may work one week with a producer who favours the 'live' approach to recording — perhaps the band have been in rehearsal long enough to get in and play all at once, as practised in the early days of recorded sound. However, with the equipment available these days it's possible to do a series of live 'takes' and replace, mix, patch where necessary the parts that don't come up to standard. The next week he may work with a producer who favours the slightly lengthier layered approach to recording — laying each track down individually, starting with the rhythm, which may go down onto as many as 12 tracks — enormous emphasis is placed on the rhythm, which forms the meat of any record. Individual tracks may be devoted to the snare, the bass drum, the hi-hat, the cymbals, etc.

The main problem encountered with this latter recording approach (now by far the most common) is bored musicians, hanging around while the technicians get the sound 'just so', tuning the drums to studio exactness and miking everything up. By the time they've finished pulling the song down to its basics, electronically and musically, and by the time they've made the musicians play pieces of it over and again for just the right 'take', some people may be sincerely hoping they'll never hear it again, in any form. Here the studio engineer, in the absence of a diplomatic producer, must be the sociable, enthusiastic, easy-going father-figure, who keeps spirits up when things are looking black. Those years of working as a tea-boy and tape op now stand him in enormously good stead. To the band he is working with, the life-style may seem new, and is undoubtedly tiring, but the studio engineer knows no other by now. He is capable of turning out work to a high standard at any time of the day or night.

It's as important for the studio engineer to build up a reputation for himself as it is for the producer, as mentioned previously, he is usually credited on the back of album covers, and it is very much down to him to pull clients in to his studio. Whenever a band book time at a particular studio, they are asked which engineer they would like to work with, and it's here that each engineer must have proved himself in the past, so that his services are requested again. A large studio with several engineers will actually encourage quite strong competition between them, so that it's up to them to find, nurture and keep hold of their own special clients, or musicians. They will also fight to be the special side-man of the independent producers — many of these prefer to work in a team with an engineer who knows what they want, and who they can trust and get along with easily.

When a studio engineer has built up a good, well-known collection of clients he may wish to go independent himself, so giving himself the freedom to negotiate his own salary instead of being bound by the studio retainer plus recording extras, which may provide a guaranteed income but not quite so financially rewarding. The independent recording engineer is also free to go out on the road as a sound engineer for his studio clients. The transition from a good recording studio mixing desk to the similar but much smaller desks taken out on the road is an easy one, and many bands favour the idea of keeping their own special man with them at all times, whether on the road or in the studio.

Many recording engineers are happy to stay just that, but many more aspire to production, when they can work better hours for a much better slice of the cake. This comes eventually when they have built themselves up to the level where bands are happy to have them producing their albums, with a credit and a royalty for so doing, and when better quality bands start to demand their services. It's a long road, and if you've tried to keep a private life going on the outside during these hard years, you've probably failed, unless you can persuade the studio you work for that your partner would be ideal to work with you, handling the studio bookings, which is a career in itself.

The Maintenance Engineer

All studios have a full-time staff of maintenance engineers, who are obsessed with all things electronic and have a side-interest in music — or sound. During a visit to a well-known studio in London, a curious onlooker wondered why instead of the expected sound of music emanating from the control rooms, there were intense discussions in unintelligible jargon, and trails of sweet-smelling smoke. It turned out that the studio was expecting the arrival of non other than John McLaughlin, perfectionist guitarist of Mahavishnu Orchestra fame, and the entire team of maintenance engineers had been set to work on the mixing desk with their soldering irons, so that not a wire would be out of place for the big occasion.

Most parts of mixing desks etc can actually be removed for maintenance quite easily, for speedy repair without affecting the whole. This can often still be used without its one input or output section, or whatever has broken down. Most studio engineers are past masters at calmly stopping a session, even when a great take has just happened, saying, 'Sorry guys, you were slightly out of tune on that one — or the bass guitarist missed a beat . . .' when in fact the channel he's just tried to record it through has shown itself to be faulty. It doesn't happen too often, and it keeps the reputation of the studio intact. Studio equipment is so specialised and the demands made on it are so great that to rely on an outside firm to put faults to right would be incredibly impracticable — far better to employ as many people as are needed to keep the equipment up to scratch on the premises.

Maintenance engineers are usually highly qualified — a degree in physics, electronics or at the very least a City and Guilds Certificate in electronic engineering is required. This is not surprising, as the technology is some of the most advanced in the world. Many of these engineers build up reputations of their own, and go off to build special recording or mixing equipment. Some of the major sound companies were started by just such people, and the industry is kept firmly up to date by their constant innovative approach which imaginative musicians only too readily appreciate.

The Cutting Engineer

Transferring sound so carefully recorded and mixed from master tape to master disc is a fairly exact process. Many of the larger studios have their own cutting rooms and equipment, or the master disc may be cut at the factory where the record is to be pressed. The engineer who oversees the cutting process is known as the cutting engineer, and it's up to this person to produce the final sound that is going to be heard on the record.

Anyone who has listened to a record via the 24-track master tape on huge studio monitors (quite an experience for a music lover) knows that it bears absolutely no resemblance at all to the final sound reproduced on a stereo album, whatever quality equipment it's played on. It's actually a well-known trap that many inexperienced bands fall into the first few times they record — they produce something which sounds terrific through the studio monitors, but rather disappointing in its finished form. Producer Mike Howlett, writing some sound advice in the same *ZigZag* feature mentioned earlier, comments on this problem, 'Try to hear the rough mixes away from the studio. Listening to it on a domestic hi-fi is the most telling test as it is easy to be fooled by the high-powered studio monitors, and, after all, most people won't be hearing it in such splendour. A good mix should present the musical idea in its most effective form. It's important to keep in mind the original idea that first inspired the song.'

The art of the cutting engineer, then, is to translate the finished sophistication of the flat-inch master tape via special cutting room monitors, onto a piece of lacquer which will form the basis for the vinyl record. A diamond-tipped cutting lathe makes the grooves in the lacquer, and the cutting engineer can alter the final sound considerably during this process — even by altering the width of the grooves, which will affect loudness. This piece of lacquer is then sent to the record plant (if it's not there already) where a negative impression is made of both sides onto thin metal which is incorporated into a stamping machine. This literally stamps grooves onto soft vinyl, along (in most cases) with the centre label, in one process. A final mechanical cutter trims the round edge, and the record is sleeved and bagged into preprinted sleeves and sent to the warehouse for collection by distribution vans to take to the shops.

So, the cutting engineer is the final link between the music and the manufactured product, vital to the success of the whole venture — a badly cut record stands out — and fails — on just that basis. He, or she, is representing the interests of the people who will buy the record and hear it on their small record players. It's no good telling the disappointed record buyer that it 'sounded alright in the studio' — you can't cram thousands of fans into a small recording studio to hear your potential, it should have been faithfully represented on that rather expensive piece of vinyl.

The cutting engineer has been through exactly the same learning process as has the recording engineer — tea-boy to tape operator. He may have tried out the mixing desk for a while, but decided that a life in the cutting room was preferable, and set about persuading the studio to let him spend some time there. Formal qualifications are the same as for the recording engineer but there is slightly less contact with the musicians. The job is usually quicker than the recording process, so that the relationship between cutting engineer and recording engineer may be fairly likened to that of a surgeon and doctor. Both have the interests of the same patient in mind, and both are vital to the health and well-being of the patient, but the surgeon experiences less patient contact, and therefore is less under the risk of late-night emotional traumas.

Studio Administration

A studio is a business, like any other, and although a great deal of its success is dependent on the good reputation of its equipment and technical staff, it's also true to say that behind every fully-booked studio is a hard-working administrator. He or she keeps in constant touch with the record and management companies, finds out which bands are likely to be requiring studio time and keeps the schedules as organised as is possible in this inefficient, spur-of-the-moment world. If a band pulls out leaving a week of empty studio time, a really good administrator should be able to find a replacement without too much difficulty. At the top end of the studio range there is much competition for the attention of quality bands. (Some can afford to pay as much as £30 per hour for the very best service, although it should be mentioned here that a perfectly good eight-track studio can be booked for as little as £7.00 per hour.)

Often the full-time booking administrator has begun life as an efficient secretary, working for the studio manager, or as an efficient receptionist and has proved her worth there.

Case Study

Colin Green is a recording engineer at Trident Studios; his good humour, patience and advice have contributed much to the production of this chapter.

> I took some O and A levels at school and, when I left, began a hotel and catering course. I was working in a bar in the evenings, and one evening I met a recording engineer. This meeting decided me that this was what I wanted to do. I wrote to every studio and managed to obtain a couple of interviews.
>
> The reason why I was successful in finding a job was that I turned up dressed in a suit. This impressed the studio manager who thought I must be really dedicated, because I looked as if I were taking the job seriously, and because I had actually been keen enough to buy a suit.
>
> I started off as a tea-boy, and worked my way up from tape operator to recording engineer, by the age of 25.
>
> Although I started off without any formal training, now there are some colleges that include studio training in their courses.

Chapter 6

The Promoter

Introduction

Promoting isn't just something you can go out and do, without prior experience or the right kind of contacts to help you. But as is so often the case in the music industry, there's no course you can attend at your local technical college which will help — except maybe business studies or law. Ask many professional promoters how they started, and they'll scratch their heads and say 'a series of accidents, I happened to be in the right place at the right time . . .'.

Needless to say, there aren't many independent promoters around — like agents, they can be counted on the fingers of one and a bit hands. But there are hundreds of promoters around the country attached to small venues, from converted country barns to thriving night clubs. Of course, what the promoter won't say when you ask him for the true ending of his sentence above is that when the right opportunity came along for him, he responded in the right way, with enthusiasm, good sense and nerves of steel. Those same opportunities, thrown in the direction of the wrong person, may have fallen on hard ground.

Is there money in promoting? Certainly, on some levels — no one can deny that an open air event which may attract 50 to 60 thousand people will make large sums of money. Of course, those masses won't turn up to watch just any old act, and the kind of acts around who can draw those numbers in will expect a large percentage of the gate receipts for their trouble. So too will the army of professionals who have to be brought in to build the stage, handle the sound and lights, the security, the people who provide facilities (imagine if all 60,000 want to relieve themselves of their light refreshments at the same time) and the ticket and poster printers. It's also worth pointing out here that not so many people turn out to open air events any more. Perhaps the advent of video has something to do with this, and in any case it rains too often in Great Britain to make this kind of promoting anything more than a bad risk. Only the heavy metal fans still consistently find it worth-while to attend such events.

The literal meaning of a promoter is someone who 'helps forward or initiates' a process. This could be any-thing from a car launching to a band in a pub — a good promoter should be able to handle either event. The key word is *initiate*, however, promoting is totally self-starting; *You* must find the venue, find the acts to fill it and then find the audience to come and pay your ticket price. Many people complain bitterly that there just isn't enough entertainment in their area — maybe a small country village, or an outpost of a city. What they should realise is that they have the power to make their own entertainment. It doesn't take very much initiative to hire a hall, whether it's the backroom of a local pub or attached to the local church. Local talent would be only too happy to have some rehear-sal time there, for a percentage of the 'door' takings, and it's not too much trouble to rig up a simple disco — there are lots of energy-filled people around who would enjoy this.

A regular disco may raise enough money eventually to hire a proper band. You're unlikely to get a 'name' band into your village hall, however, no matter how much money there is in the kitty to pay for them. If you've read the rest of this book thoroughly you'll have worked out by now that a band with any kind of a 'name' to protect is going to do itself no good at all playing in out-of-the-way village, or college halls. When it's single-selling time, only the most publicly available venues are sought after — the ones in the largest radio catchment area, for interviews before and after the gig, in cities where the record shops can be approached during the tour to put up cardboard displays. It's not the number of people who attend the gigs who count to those bands and their record companies, but the number of people who *hears* about the gigs — the amount of brouhaha which surrounds them.

The Difference between Promoters

Every year a few people with more money than sense appear in the music world with schemes for events at football stadiums involving the Rolling Stones or the Pink Floyd. Journalists on trade papers come into contact with them first, when they ring up to ask for the phone numbers of the Rolling Stones management office. They're known by the collective name of 'Wally Promotions', and there's the odd agent or two who will take them for a few dates, money up front — although less and less are prepared to even take their phone calls these days. Nowadays, reputation counts for more and more — if you're known for your dealings with Wally Promotions, don't expect anyone else to have anything to do with you. But what's the difference between Wally Promotions and any other promotion company? About ten years, usually. Ten years of finding out the hard way which p.a. company can supply the best and most efficient sound systems, which trucking companies supply spare trucks within 24 hours of breakdown anywhere in Europe, which tour managers won't have nervous breakdowns half-way through a tour and which independent promoters won't run away with the door receipts on the night.

Imagine you're a huge, world-famous heavy metal act who have a guaranteed pulling power of at least 50,000 ardent fans even to a swamp in the Southern States of America. You can choose which promoter you want to handle your next few public appearances. A millionaire with no contacts or experience approaches you — he wants you to play an untested football stadium somewhere in the Midlands. He's got no idea when your next album is due out — actually the date he offers you is a month before the release date so that even if all goes well you won't sell any albums. Then a well-known promoter approaches you. He's in close contact with the record company, your management company, and although he's not offering so much 'silly' money — more likely he's offering a good percentage. The performances will be in tried and tested venues, and will coincide with your album release, so that you can go out and do all sorts of radio and television promotion in the cities you visit. You know this second promoter — you've worked with him on a few past tours and he's always looked after you well, smoothing frayed tempers in the early hours of the morning and supplying the most experienced crew and merchandising companies. Who would you do business with — the professional who can do your career the most good, or the 'get rich quick' chancer who, by just one stupid mistake, could destroy your career at a stroke?

How to Begin as a Promoter

A good few of the professional promoters around began life as the social secretary at their local college or university. Of course, social secretaries have to make a success of their year to show their worth. Running through the larger promoters around at the moment who started life as social secretaries, it's true to say that they practically earned themselves a golden plaque from their grateful colleges, so imaginative and profitable were their years in office. It's also worth noting that they didn't go straight into professional promoting — without exception they all spent a while (some longer than others) in an agency office, learning the business from the professional side. How many of those promoters still work with colleges? Actually, none — professional promoters these days just don't have the time or the energy to work with amateur promoters, particularly in colleges, who may have a reputation for signing contracts right, left and centre, with little or no intention of actually going out and 'promoting' the date with all that that entails.

There are just a few college venues which have the right facilities and — more importantly — permanent entertainment officers who can be relied upon to provide the right atmosphere and the right audience for the bands they promote, as any professional promoter would be expected to do. There is too much of a feeling on the college circuit that somehow because they have the money (and they do), and the hall, the rest of the music industry owes them a living. A 17-year-old student, fresh to his social secretary post, is to be regarded as suspect, he is inexperienced and certainly does not have the best interests of the band at heart. Usually he knows nothing of his predecessor's year. Each year, the poor frustrated agent is faced with a whole batch of new social secretaries who may not even know his telephone number, despite the fact that he may have been exclusively booking their college the previous year, having worked and scraped to build up a good working relationship with the then social secretary, and maybe even to build up the college as a respectable venue.

Students have changed their role as an audience over the last ten years — whereas once it was on the college circuit that a band made its reputation — students were musically very aware, bought albums and attended lots of concerts, now it's the non-student population that makes up the bulk of the 'fans'. Students, in these troubled times, are more concerned with obtaining qualifications. When May Ball time comes around, they want to be entertained, not educated. It's worth remembering that if you're a college promoter trying to choose between a chart act or an old faithful for your ball. The chart act might be good for your image, but the old faithful will be better for your bank balance and your audience.

If you're really keen to make a success of your year, perhaps you can allow members of the public into your hall, few bands like the elitist 'students only' ruling at most colleges, it means that their fans in the college catchment area can't come to see them.

It's also well worth your while making out a list of the best agencies and spending a couple of days going to visit them in their respective lairs, befriending them and showing them that it's worth *their* while spending some time on your venue. They don't owe you a living, by any means, but if you can convince them that all concerned may actually *make* a good living, then you'll be guaranteed a good hearing at the very least. The same rule applies to anyone wanting to start promoting from scratch, whether it's in a village hall or the back room of a pub. If you're going to be dealing with those acts who have agency representation, then you'll have to form some kind of relationship — preferably friendly — with the people you'll be relying upon for your living.

Case Study

Paul Crockford is a music fan. He considers that if he wasn't a promoter, he'd be going to exactly the same number of gigs anyway, so he regards himself as lucky to be doing something which is an extension of his main hobby and interest. He was a social secretary at university, but is one of those professional promoters who reckons to have been 'in the right place at the right time' when the opportunities came along. He worked as a tour manager for a medium-range pop band, and this involved waiting around the agency/promotion office during the off-hours. Eventually that office offered him a job going out on the road with some of the bands they were promoting. He has stayed with that promotion company ever since, now enjoying a directorship and taking pride in the fact that he has been involved in its build up from a company which handled almost exclusively 'heavy metal' bands, to one which looks forward to five dates at Wembley Arena this year with a world-famous band.

He attributes the company's success to hard work, persistence, and a reputation for involving itself in a band's career from the start, instead of organising money-grabbing tours for a few certainties each year.

> The music industry has reached such a point that you really do need a good reputation behind you before a band with any pulling power will even speak to you. Most of the bands we promote at the moment have worked with us for several years. We have built up a good relationship and taken care to

be very selective about the venues we promote them in with each successive tour. If you really want to make a success of a promoting career, you have to think in the long term. It may be worth your while in the short term, for example, to add an extra Hammersmith Odeon date for a band who have already sold out the first four advertised. But in the long term that's really bad for business. If the band is overexposed one year, it will be almost impossible to sell them anywhere the next year. That works on every level — not just at the top end of the market. If a promoter can become involved with the career of the band when they're relatively new, then he's more likely to be able to move with them into the bigger venues as they progress up the scale.

A lot of promoters are terribly out of touch — they are at the centre of a very insular business, and have their views shaped by maybe half a dozen people who are supposedly 'in the know'. To those half dozen people, some band might be the next big thing, but if that promoter went and asked someone in the streets of Newcastle, he'd probably have never even heard of that band — and isn't likely to spend his hard-earned money going to see them.

Obviously there's a hard core of rock fans who keep themselves well-informed — those people fill the smaller clubs without fail. But successful promoting nowadays has to pull in the schoolgirl who may have to persuade her parents to let her go to a concert — or even to accompany her — and the fan who gets his information from Top of the Pops. That's where the art comes in; personally I read the music papers from cover to cover every week without fail. I go to enormous numbers of shows and speak to as many people there as possible; I listen to records, and the radio — so finding out what's going on. You can't let up on that kind of contact if you want to stay in the business.

The industry's reliance on 'reputation' isn't as elitist as it sounds — it's really a kind of safety net. If you work with someone who's been doing successful promotions for about ten years, say, then you're much less likely to get 'knocked' than if you work with someone who's only just appeared. That's not totally foolproof, however, even as I speak there are two major promotion companies going into liquidation, and many people who worked with them have lost out seriously. But those people will work again, with the same people — because they know each other so well. That's particularly important in Europe, where we rely upon a few familiar and trusted promoters for almost everything.

It's sad to say that in Great Britain the music industry isn't as respected as it is, say, in the States. Over here — partly for that reason, promoting is much more low-key. I find myself coming up against members of my family asking me, 'Have you got a proper job yet?', as if the success I've made of my career in the music industry was somehow value-less. In America, if I was doing the same thing, my family would be delighted. It's far more establishment in America, and has far more respect. There isn't so much money in promoting here, it's true — but there could be, with careful management and a much more professional attitude.

Chapter 7
The Roadie

Introduction

If you're thinking about joining the road crew of a famous band — starting at the bottom of course — if you're the type to whom the gypsy life of the roadie appeals, I won't have to spend time telling you about the appalling hours, the low wages, the hours, days and months you may have to spend in the back of a van bumping your way up and down the highways of Europe. This is followed by the hours of waiting around with nothing to do at venues, being hassled by amateur promoters and idiots. Perhaps you've listened to the lyrics of 'The Load Out' by Jackson Browne and Brian Garofalo from the 'Running on Empty' album, released in 1978 on Elektra/Asylum Records. It starts:

> *Now the seats are all empty*
> *Let the Roadies take the stage*
> *Pack it up and tear it down.*
> *They're the first to come and the last to leave*
> *Working for that minimum wage*
> *They'll set it up in another town.*
> *Tonight the people were so fine*
> *They waited there in line*
> *And when they got up on their feet they made the show*
> *And that was sweet — But I can hear the sound*
> *Of slamming doors and folding chairs*
> *And that's a sound they'll never know.*
> *Now roll them cases out and lift them amps*
> *Haul them trusses down and get 'em up them ramps*
> *'Cause when it comes to moving me*
> *You guys are the champs . . .*   (©1977 Warner Bros Music Ltd)

It's a fine ode to the roadie, who, when he's doing his job well is truly the unsung hero of the show. But he's earned that accolade the hardest way possible, and despite the undisputed romance attached to his work, there still has to be a particular kind of personality which can withstand the dreadful life and even enjoy it.

Few roadies have successful home lives — if they're any good, they're out on the road nine months of the year, and there's no way they'll be allowed to bring the wife and children along. From the wife's point of view, it's not like being married to a submariner who's at sea all the time he's away — roadies are hanging around at gigs, meeting a wide variety of girls. An experienced roadie whose seen more backstage scenes than he cares to remember doesn't find it too difficult to resist temptation, but a younger roadie is more likely to succumb. There are many long hours to fill when he's just waiting around; a passion for Russian novels or Solitaire would be an advantage.

In addition, the life isn't too good for the constitution. Food consists of whatever the hotel can unwillingly rustle up at three o'clock in the morning (when the roadie's day finishes), or something — usually chips — hastily eaten in a motorway restaurant. How many years of stress, boredom and poor food can he withstand, before perching at the top of a 20-foot ladder focusing coloured lights becomes too much of a strain on the system?

There's no union in this country. The States are well organised in that respect, unionised crews look after each other with loving care, but touring over there is a much more expensive proposition as a result. The flexibility which the total lack of unionisation in this country allows is a boon at the lower end of the touring market — a band which must change their schedule, play later, or whose transport perhaps breaks down on the motorway needn't have to worry about paying massive wages to a mercenary crew just to get the job done. They may even manage with one trusty man to handle their rigging, lighting and sound problems — something a union would never allow. The argument for a union is strong — better wages, better hours and less exploitation, not to say more respect for the specialised roadie as a craftsman in his own right, with skills and expertise which would have been unknown 20 years ago. Perhaps for this reason the establishment has been only too slow to respond with courses at technical colleges, tied to proper apprenticeships with lighting and sound companies.

The Job Difficulties

At the moment the young 'trainee' roadie — perhaps an enthusiastic yet non-musical friend of an up-and-coming band — has to rely on the weather eye of his more experienced colleagues to literally keep him alive at times. That may sound a little overdramatic, but most acts these days use literally huge amounts of electricity, with rigs and systems which have become more and more complicated. Older roadies, bearing in mind past experiences and even tragedies, are increasingly safety conscious as well they might be. A famous horror story which is told is of two young roadies gazing at a burning plug, wondering what to do. 'Let's throw a bucket of water over it,' suggested one, but luckily for him he was physically restrained by a third crew member before he could do too much damage. Everyone hears stories of guitarists who electrocute themselves with badly-earthed mikes and guitars, but less people hear about the roadies who fall down stage-traps in darkened theatres, or off rigging and ladders.

It's a highly skilled job, and as well as a cheerful disposition and a sound constitution, an aptitude for electrical and electronic equipment is a basic requirement. An HGV licence is useful, although more and more trucking companies are using their own drivers whose specific task is driving and humping. On a small scale, HGV licences are not really a necessity — a clean licence is the only useful aid.

Being a roadie is like everything else in the music business — if you are prepared to start at the bottom with a local hopeful band, and to keep your eyes and ears open and learn from the others around you, then if you are any good at your job the word will soon get around. In most cases, you are as good as the last band you worked for.

Case Study

Nick Bell is a lighting man, through and through. He's worked with just about everyone you can think of, including acts like King Crimson in the early seventies when the lighting practically took over the whole show. King Crimson were famous as much for their extravagant psychedelic lights as they were for their music, and many acts nowadays would love to recreate that visual aspect of their live show. He has his own small rig and works alone through what he terms 'eccentric choice' although he acknowledges the value of the large lighting companies, particularly as regards the training of young lighting men.

I was lucky when I began, because lighting men really were a rare commodity and finding work wasn't too hard. My interest in lights started as far back as the sixties when I became involved with the lights for a local art school disco. It was very simple — a few slides and projectors; I was trying to produce a multi-media show and actually change what was happening around me with regard to kinetic colour forms. That show was what decided me. Together with my brother, (who hasn't remained in the business) I brought the show to quite a high level of technique — it was very sophisticated. That lasted about two years — we ended up taking it around the country with a little band and hiring ourselves out to other bands for not very much money.

Things changed, however, my artist friend who had helped me in the beginning went back to his painting, my brother was married and I was asked to handle the stage lighting for Wishbone Ash, who were quite big news at the time. At that stage, bands hardly used proper light shows at all — a few theatre spots usually sufficed, and it was just the beginning of that era when bands started actually thinking about light shows. They paid me a wage — I think it was about £11 per week and gave me a budget to go and hire the lights from an established company, which I then put together into a show, all on my own. Each lamp had to be hung separately, scaffolding had to be put up, there was no portable lighting system then as there is today. It was very hard work, for little or no money, and after a few years of that I found I just couldn't survive in London any longer — I was literally on subsistence level. I left them — very upset, because after such a long time with one band you do become very emotionally involved. On the same day I was offered a job running the lighting system of a new club in Manchester, called the Hard Rock, which had just had about a quarter of a million pounds spent on it, making it one of the best venues of its time.

Working there was invaluable for me, despite the boredom of remaining in one place all the time; but being the house lighting man there meant being able to meet lots of other lighting men and bands who came through. I learnt an enormous amount from them and also met up with old friends — King Crimson, who wanted a lighting man to go out on the road with them to America. I jumped at the chance to travel and joined the crew. For the first time I found myself working with a proper modern lighting rig, with all its built-in toys, and I look back on the two years I spent with them as my best working years. I was well paid, in a good crew with a good manager and I travelled widely — going to America no less than five times. It couldn't last for ever, though, it was the end of the King Crimson era and eventually the band broke up — we were all out of a job, quite suddenly.

I spent a few years 'in the wilderness' then — working with various lighting companies and many different bands. It was all very insecure — just as I became involved with a band I would have to move on or maybe they would split up. I decided to set myself up as an independent; I gradually bought my own lights and built up my business to the level it's at now, which is comfortably busy.

One day I could see myself becoming involved with television lighting, say — but it's so totally different to the kind of lighting that I do now that I would look on it mainly as a challenge, to see if I could work in a completely different medium, although still in lighting of course. No matter how fancy or technical lighting equipment becomes, it's still basically a light source and a way of controlling it — that's all it comes down to. You can improve on ways of hanging the lights and moving them around, and you can improve the control systems — even have computerised ones now — but at the end of the day it's the same. A sound man would agree with me as far as his equipment is concerned — you can improve on the speakers, the amplifiers, the mixing decks, but at the end of his road it's still sound, the best he can produce. It's also true to say that if the lights are superb, the sound is good, yet the band are terrible, you still have a poor show on your hands — it's the show that counts above everything.

Chapter 8

The Publisher, the Journalist and Others

The Publisher

There's one aspect of the music industry which isn't so well known as the others, although it's easier to enter (so say those in the know), and is by far the most profitable. The publishing deal signed with an unknown band is not dissimilar to that made by a record company. But whereas the record company is committed to vast departments handling press, promotions, marketing, artist-liaison, etc, the publishing company just signs the contract which guarantees it a constant percentage of the sales of a particular song, and then sits back while the record company does the work of recording and selling. Of course, for every song, songwriter or band a music publishing house takes on that goes on to sell a million records there are hundreds with publishing deals that are never even recorded or have their songs placed.

This is where the publishing company comes in useful — it will go out into the market place, and find either the right recording artist, or the right recording deal for you if you perform your own songs. It's therefore quite a good plan of action for an aspiring band who also write lots of their own, strong material, to approach the a & r man in a good, reputable publishing company to see if he can do anything to help. There are a few ex-agents to be found lurking within the corridors of music publishing companies, so they should have an eye for talent at the very least. Publishing isn't something you can go straight into without previous — usually extensive and successful — experience in the industry.

It's worth noting that you don't always have to give away your publishing rights if you are a singer/songwriter — you can go ahead and sign a record deal, retaining the publishing rights for yourself. It's extra work, chasing up those publishing royalties for yourself via the Performing Rights Society, whose computer actually does the royalty chasing, from radio, television and venues. (If someone in your local pub plays a copyright song — like 'Goodnight Eileen' — the PRS will want to know. Supposedly the pub is licensed to play music via the PRS, which collects directly off it.) If you are signed to a publishing company, the PRS send money straight to that company — it arrives with stunning regularity on your doormat each year, minus the company's percentage, sounds too easy to be true!

The Music Journalist

He's a strange breed, the music journalist. He may have come through the usual journalistic channels (a training course run by the National Council for the Training of Journalists, which includes a three-year apprenticeship on local newspapers) but had a strong ambition to work in the music business or, alternatively, he may be just a non-musical, articulate, hardy music fanatic. In this latter case, he may have sent in countless articles to music papers and magazines until at last one of them took notice of him.

A journalist, before he becomes a household name within the industry, must have enormous charm and the hide of a donkey. Time after time his hard-sweated labours of love are rejected without word or explanation from music papers. He is in competition with literally hundreds of other hopefuls at this stage. The money is not particularly good — even the most revered editor earns the basic union rate. It's also worth noting that once branded as a music journalist, you'll have trouble going back to 'straight' writing, unless you are a talented sub-editor who can transfer onto another newspaper without difficulty. The man who makes his reputation based on an expertise in reggae music should think carefully whether he wants this to be his niche for the foreseeable future.

A journalists's life is fairly energetic apart from working on your paper or magazine as a normal journalist, your news-gathering takes place late at night, watching the latest hot act in some equally hot club; take just a few weeks off and you'll find yourself slipping out of touch and out of a job. The good music journalist, like the agent, is at every venue in town. If he's not there, he's either been or he's about to arrive. In addition, he's expected to work his way through the new releases each week — singles and albums. Sounds great, if you are really a devoted music fan, but a few years of nothing but new releases, and you may find yourself begging for a holiday on a desert island with your Buddy Holly collection.

Other Professions

It's worth noting that the music industry is fairly specialist by it's nature and so requires many special services, such as the accountant who only deals with music companies, or the lawyer who has made a name for himself as a wizard with record company contracts. Many of these people find jobs inside the industry — working from within a record company as the 'in-house' lawyer or accountant, or even launching their expertise into a management project.

Commercial artists, too, may find a niche within the industry, designing record covers, picture sleeves for singles, or merchandising logos; here their eccentric creativity is welcomed rather than stifled. Many of the larger record companies have their own art departments, which are worth approaching with your portfolio if you think you have something to offer. There are also many outside studios that produce artwork both for the music industry and for other industries.

The rock photographer is someone who 'sees' music visually and will admit to watching all concerts as a series of potential shots. If your camera clicks at the right time in the right place and you can produce a good print, then there may be a place for you, either with the band themelves, their press officer or a music paper. It takes a while to build your reputation to the point where a band will ask for you when they're preparing a new set of shots for their press file, but it's a satisfying and rewarding job if you're not only good with your camera, but, like the journalist, you have a tough exterior, and a belief in yourself which is undented by rejection.

Part 2

Chapter 9

Courses and Useful Addresses

Music Courses

Huddersfield Polytechnic
Queensgate, Huddersfield HD1 3DH
BA Honours, 3 years full-time
BA Graduate diploma, 3 years full-time
Minimum entrance requirement one A level in music. Both courses include training in an electronic recording studio. There is much emphasis on practical work — the college has many bands, including brass. Most students go on to take a teaching certificate.

Leeds College of Music
Cookridge, Street, Leeds LS2 8BH
Graduate diploma in Jazz and Light Music, 3 years
Entrance requirements are four O levels and two A levels including music. The prospective student must have reached grade 8 of the Associated Board Examination in his first instrument. The course is versatile, and there is a great emphasis on the practical side of playing — the college has at least 40 different bands.

Polytechnic of North London
Holloway Road, London N7 8DB
Sound Studios and Recording, 1 year part-time
The student gains a knowledge of both the fundamental principles and techniques of the subject, to the standard required by City and Guilds course 271 part 111. An internal examination is set which is assessed and approved by the City and Guilds Institute. Entry requirements are: a successful completion of City and Guilds 271 parts 1 and 11, or ONC/OND, or A level GCE, or equivalent, in science subjects. The course is currently held on Thursday afternoons from 2.30 - 4.30 pm. Course organiser: Dr R C Driscoll

The same department also offers a 3-year full-time Honours degree course in electronics and communications, with a full final year option in audio engineering and acoustics.

Newcastle upon Tyne College of Arts
Maple Terrace, Newcastle upon Tyne NE4 7SA
Diploma in Light Music, 3 years
Professional Music diploma, 3 years
A generous approach to recruitment in searching for musical talent, rather than an excess of formal qualifications. The two basic groups of entrants encompass school-leavers who already play an instrument, and who have had possibly some kind of formalised training, and want a musical education slanted towards popular music, and slightly older recruits who may have been part-time musicians, and now want to take time out to study their instrument properly, whether it be the bass guitar, keyboards, saxophone or whatever. For those without a musical background (formal) there is a foundation course which will put them in a position to handle the formal aspects of the diplomas. The foundation course falls into four broad areas.

1. It is suitable for people who may want to find a job in one of the large firms around the North, for whom a vital requirement is the ability to join the firm's brass band.
2. There is a course in the performing arts for non-musician dancers and actors who wish to find work in stage shows — they can take O levels in drama or music appreciation as well as studying dancing, tap, music and singing.
3. There is a normal foundation course in preparation for the diplomas, when the student may take O or A levels in music.
4. There is a special module for the student who wants an entry into popular music but has no traditional training at all — basically a crash course programme.

The professional music diploma is a modular course — 3 years of working with your principal instrument in a full-time musical atmosphere, as well as at least one other instrument. A personal learning programme is developed for each student which may include subsidiary subjects like arts administration or orchestration.

The light music diploma — is of 3 years' duration at the music school, learning first and second instruments as well as arranging, jazz improvisation etc.

There is also a part-time course in which the above diplomas can be converted to a BA. Head of the School of Music: Mr Jim Joseph

Salford College of Technology
Music Section, Adelphi Building, Peru Street, Salford
Advanced college diploma in Band Musicianship. Three options: graduate, professional popular music and recording techniques, 3 years full-time minimum age 18

Foundation courses
Three options: academic — O and A levels in music, professional, popular music and recording techniques, 2 years, minimum age 16.

Entry to the foundation course in popular music and recording techniques is by audition, and successful completion enables students to transfer to the advanced diploma course. The purpose at this level is to improve the musical literacy of the students by working on theory, history, aural, keyboard harmony and element-ary techniques, while incorporating a strong practical content with substantial recording studio experience. The popular music option of the advanced diploma is intended for students who wish to reach a professional standard of musicianship for performance, 'session' work etc. Students study harmony, aural, history (including jazz and commercial music), keyboard harmony, scoring and arranging, first and second study instrumental lessons, recording technology and relevant ancillary studies.

Advanced certificate in South Recording Technology and Techniques, 3 years full-time
Intended to train maintenance engineers for the recording industry. Successful students receive a professional technician's certificate.
Lecturer in charge of Popular Music Studies: A J Cliff BMus(Hons) FLCM Cert Ed

University of Surrey
Guildford, Surrey
Tonmeister BMus, 4 years
This course includes one year in the recording industry. Combines physics, electronics and music, including music composition and performance. Stiff entrance requirements, including physics and music A levels at grade B, and maths at grade C. Musical entrance requirements are grade 8 Associated Board in the first instrument — great emphasis is placed on keyboards training; there is a keyboards exam at the end of the first year. Considered by the Association of Professional Recording Studios to be the *Crème de la Crème* of courses available.
Course head: Professor Forbes

Courses in Performance Arts

IM March College of Education
Barkhill Road, Liverpool 17
CNAA BA, 3 years full-time

Leicester Polytechnic
Dopt Try, PO Box 143
Leicester LE1 9BH
CNAA BA, 3 years full-time

Middlesex Polytechnic
114 Chase Side, London N14 5PN
CNAA BA, 3 years full-time

Nonington College of Further Education
Nonington, Nr Dover, Kent
BA, 3 years full-time

Courses usually include drama, dance and music. Apply to individual colleges for details.

Short Courses

Wavendon Allmusic Plan
The Stables, Wavendon, Milton Keynes MK17 8LT
Runs a variety of short music courses throughout the year for all ages, ranging from short master classes of an hour or so's duration to residential events lasting about a week. Some, such as Avril Dankworth's National Music Camps, are specially planned to cater for children and young people. The courses at present are:
WAP Easter allmusic course
WAP summer jazz course
WAP winter classical course
Avril Dankworth National Music Camps
WAP master classes and workshops
JWAP junior workshops.

Agencies

The Agency, Premier House, 150 Southampton Row, London WC1B 5AY; 01-278 3331

Asgard, 155-7 Oxford Street, London W1; 01-734 3426

Ann Dex, 1a Montagu Mews North, London W1H 1AU; 01-935 0413

Bankhouse Entertainments, 11a Victoria Square, Holmfirth, Huddersfield; 048-489 2255

Big Bear, 190 Monument Road, Birmingham 16; 021-454 7020

Carousel Artistes, Amber House, 278 Seven Sisters Road, London N4; 01-272 9122

Concorde Agency, First Floor, Southbank House, Black Prince Road, London SE1 7SJ; 01-735 8171

Cowbell Agency, 153 George Street, London W1H 5LB; 01-262 7253

Derek Block Artistes Agency, 1 Richmond Mews, Richmond Buildings, Dean Street, London W1; 01-439 6521

Handle Artistes, 1 Derby Street, London W1; 01-493 9637

International Talent Booking, 113-117 Wardour Street, London W1V 3TD; 01-439 8041

John Sherry Entertainments, 6 Cavendish Court, 11 Wigmore Street, London W1A 9LB; 01-409 1299

Kicking Mule Agency (Folk), 125 Studderidge Street, Fulham, London SW6; 01-736 4570

Mecca Agency, 14 Oxford Street, London W1; 01-637 9401

Performing Artists Network, 10 Sutherland Avenue, London W9 2QH 01-289 6161

Promotion and Management International Limited, 6 Duke Street, Manchester Square, London W1; 01-487 5075

Ronnie Scott Productions, 47 Frith Street, London W1; 01-439 7791

Rough Trade Booking, 137 Blenheim Crescent, London W11; 01-221 2761

Smash Artists, 55a Yeldham Road, London W6; 10-741 7836

TBA International Ltd, 170 Kings Road, London SW3; 01-351 5235

Stallion Artists, 76 Roebuck House, Stag Place, London SW1; 01-828 0227

Station Agency, 41 North Road, London N7 9DP; 01-607 9577

Terry King Associates, 9-11 Monmouth Street, London WC2; 01-836 4761

Upright Artists, 49-52 Kensington Gardens Square, London W2; 01-229 8856

Wasted Talent, 28 Alexander Street, London W2; 01-221 6136

Directories

Circuit Rock Directory, 20 Fairlawn Court, Acton Lane, London W4; 01-995 3029

Entertainment Event, That's Entertainment, Cabin V, 25 Horsell Road, London N5; 01-607 4492

Kemps International Music and Recording Yearbook, The Kemps Group, 1-5 Bath Street, London EC1V 9QA; 01-253 4761

Music and Video Week Yearbook, 40 Long Acre, London WC2; 01-836 1522

Record and Tape Directory, Parkway Publications Ltd, Linburn House, 350 High Road, London NW6; 01-328 3344

Record Business Small Labels Catalogue, Hyde House, 13 Langley Street, London WC2H 9JG; 01-836 9311

Showcall (published by *The Stage and Television Today*), Stage House, 47 Bermondsey Street, London Bridge, London SE1; 01-403 1818

Magazines and Periodicals

Beat Instrumental, 18 Parkfield Street, London N1; 01-359 5419

Billboard (US Version of Music Week), 7 Carnaby Street, London W1; 01-437 8090

Black Echoes, 113 High Holborn, London WC1V 7JJ; 01-405 0461

Black Music, 23-34 Heynott Street, London SE1; 01-402 7708

Blues and Soul, 153 Praed Street, London W2; 01-402 6869

Broadcast, 111a Wardour Street, London W1V 3TD; 01-439 9756

Campaign (advertising industry trade paper), 22 Lancaster Gate, London W2; 01-402 4200

Circuit (agents' and promoters' trade paper), 20 Fairlawn Court, Acton Lane, London W4; 01-995 3029

Club and Institute Journal, 158 Buckingham Palace Road, London SW1; 01-730 9076

Club Mirror, 18 Queens Road, Brighton, Sussex; 0271 24238

Club Secretary, United Trade Press Limited, 33-5 Bowling Green Lane, London EC1; 01-837 1212

Disco International, 37 Foley Street, London W1; 01-637 1163

Entertainment and Arts Management Magazine, (civic promoters' trade paper), John Offord (Publications) Ltd, PO Box 64, Eastbourne, East Sussex; 0323 37841

Folk Review, Austin House, Hospital Street, Nantwich, Cheshire; 0272 65542

Guitar, 20 Denmark Street, London WC2H 3NA; 01-836 2326

International Musician and Recording World, Grosvenor House, 141-3 Drury Lane, London WC2; 01-379 6917

Jazz Times, British Jazz Society, 10 Southfield Gardens, Twickenham, Middlesex; 01-892 0133

Melody Maker, 168-73 High Holborn, London WC1; 01-379 3581

Music and Video Week (major industry trade paper), 40 Long Acre, London WC2; 01-836 1522

New Musical Express, Third Floor, 5-7 Carnaby Street, London W1; 01-439 8761

Night Out (Southern England event magazine), 87 Gloucester Road, Brighton, Sussex; 0273 692682

Publican (Maclaren Publishers), PO Box 109, 69-77 High Street, Croydon CR9 1QH; 01-688 7788

Record Business (major industry trade paper), Hyde House, 13 Langley Street, London WC2H 9JG; 01-836 9311

Record Mirror, 40 Long Acre, Covent Garden, London WC2E 9JT; 01-836 1522

Rolling Stone, Spotlight Publications, Spotlight House, 1 Benwell Road, London N7; 01-733 4444

South International, Link House Group, Dingwall Avenue, Croydon CR9 2TA; 01-686 2599

Sounds, 40 Long Acre, Covent Garden, London WC2E 9JT; 01-836 1522

The Stage and Television Today, Stage House, 47 Bermondsey Street, London Bridge, London SE1; 01-403 1818

Studio Sound, Link House Group, Dingwall Avenue, Croydon CR9 2TA; 10-686 2599

Time Out (London event magazine), Tower House, Southampton Street, London WC2; 01-836 4411

ZigZag, London House, 266 Fulham Road, London SW10 9EL; 01-352 3044

Record Companies

Albion Records Ltd, 147 Oxford Street, London W1; 01-734 9072

A & M Records, 136-50 New Kings Road, London SW3; 01-736 3311

Ariola/Arista Records, 3 Cavendish Square, London W1; 01-580 5566

Automatic Records, 5 Avery Row, London W1; 01-483 9744

Beggars Banquet Records, 8 Hogarth Road, London SW5; 01-370 6175

BBC Records and Tapes, The Langham, Portland Place, London W1; 01-580 4468

Big Bear Records, 190 Monument Road, Birmingham B16 8UU; 021-454 7020

Black Mountain Records, PO Box 207, Mumbles, Swansea; 0792 61234

Bonaparte Records, 101 George Street, Croydon, Surrey; 01-681 3062

Broadside Records, Studley House, 68 Limes Road, Tettenhall, Wolverhampton; 0902 753047

Bronze Records, 100 Chalk Farm Road, London NW1 8EH; 01-267 4499

BTW Recorded Music Library, 125 Myddleton Road, London N22; 01-886 6655

Calendar Records, 89 Chiswick High Road, London W4; 01-995 3682

Carrere Records (UK), Meadow House, 22 Queen Street, Mayfair, London W1; 01-493 7406

Cavalcade Records, 138 New Bond Street, London W1Y 9FB; 01-493 9681

CBS Records, 17/19 Soho Square, London W1V 6HE; 01-734 8181

Charisma Records, 90 Wardour Street, London W1; 01-434 1351

Charly Music, 9 Beadon Road, London W6; 01-741 0011

Cherry Red Records Ltd, 53 Kensington Gardens Square, London W2; 01-229 8854

Chiswick Records, 9 Kentish Town Road, London NW1; 01-267 5192

Chrysalis Records, 12 Stratford Place, London W1; 01-408 2355

CMC Records, 14 New Burlington Street, London W1; 01-734 3251

Coast Records, The Music Works Studios, 23 Benwell Road, London, N7; 01-609 1091

Conifer Records, Horton Road, West Drayton, Middlesex, 81 49140

Crass Records, 10 Myddleton Road, London N22; 01-889 6166

Creole Records, 91-3 High Street, Harlesden, London NW10; 01-965 9223

Criminal Records, 498-500 Harrow Road, London W9; 01-960 5578

Decca Records (UK), 50 New Bond Street, London W1; 01-491 4600

DinDisc, 61-3 Portobello Road, London W11; 01-221 7535

DJM Records, James House, 5-11 Theobalds Road, London WC1; 01-242 6886

Do-It Records, PO Box 403, London NW1; 01-486 3602

Emerald Records, 120 Coach Road, Templepatrick, Ballyclare, Co Antrim; 084 94 32711

EMI Records, EMI House, 20 Manchester Square, London, W1; 01-486 4488

Ensign Records, 44 Seymour Place, London W1; 01-723 8464

4-AD Records, 8 Hogarth Road, London SW5; 01-370 6175

Fast Product and Tune Noise, 3 East Norton Place, Abbeyhill, Edinburgh; 031-229 3159

Faulty Products, 41B Blenheim Crescent, London W11 2EF; 01-727 0734

Folk Heritage Recordings, Mid Wales Sound Studios, Welshpool, Powys; 0938 82585

Graduate Records, 1 Union Street, Dudley, West Midlands DY2 8PG; 0384 59048

Greensleeves Records, 44 Uxbridge Road, Shepherds Bush, London W12; 01-749 3277

Grosvenor Records, 16 Grosvenor Road, Handsworth Wood, Birmingham B20 3NP; 021-356 9636

GTO Records, 37 Soho Square, London W1; 01-439 8971

Heavy Metal Records, 165 Wolverhampton Road, Sedgley, Dudley, West Midlands; 09073 3356

Humber Records, 49 Newmarket Street, Grimsby, South Humberside; 0472 40152

Hurricane Records, Damont Factory, Blyth Road, Hayes, Middlesex; 01-573 5122

Ice Records, 81 Osbaldeston Road, London N16; 01-806 3252

Island Records Ltd, 22 St Peter's Square, Hammersmith, London W6; 01-741 1511

Jazz Music, 7 Kildare Road, Swinton, Manchester M27 3AB; 061-794 3525

Jazz Services Unlimited, 21 Bull Green, Halifax, West Yorkshire; 0422 64773

Jet Records, 102-14 Gloucester Place, London W1; 01-486 6040

K-Tel International, 620 Western Avenue, London W3; 01-992 8000

Label Records, 106 Dawes Road, Fulham, London SW6; 01-385 5660

Lightning Records, 841 Harrow Road, Harlesdon, London NW10; 01-969 5255

Magnet Records, Magnet House, 22 York Street, London W1H 1FD; 01-486 8151

Magnum Force, 15 Albert Crescent, Penarth, Glamorgan; 0222 704279

MAM Records, 24-5 New Bond Street, London W1; 01-529 9255

MCA Records, 1 Great Pultney Street, London W1; 01-439 9951

Motown Records, 16 Curzon Street, London W1; 01-493 1603

Mountain Records, 49 Mount Street, London W1; 01-491 2904

Nimbus Records, Wyastone Leys, Monmouth, NP5 3SR; 0600 890682

Oval Records, Basement, 11 Liston Road, London SW4; 01-622 0111

Phonogram Records, 50 New Bond Street, London W1A 2BR; 01-491 4600

Pinnacle Records, Electron House, Gray Avenue, Orpington, Kent; 0689 73141

Polydor, 17/19 Stratford Place, London W1; 01-499 8686

Polygram Leisure, 15 George Street, Hanover Square, London W1; 01-499 3751

President Records, Broadmead House, 21 Panton Street, London SW1; 01-839 4672

Pye Records, ATV House, 17 Great Cumberland Place, London W1; 01-262 5502

Radar Records, 60 Parker Street, London WC2; 01-404 5832

RAK Records, 42-8 Charlbert Street, London NW8; 01-586 2012

RCA Records, 1 Bedford Avenue, London WC1; 01-499 4100

Recommended Records, 583 Wandsworth Road, London SW8; 01-622 8834

Rialto Records, 4 Yeoman's Row, London SW8; 01-584 2441

Riva Records, 2 New Kings Road, London SW6; 01-731 4131

Rockburgh Records, PO Box 283, London SW6; 01-731 3144

Rocket Records, 104 Lancaster Gate, London W2; 01-258 3585

Rola Records, Norfolk House, Well Walk, Cheltenham, Gloucestershire; 0242 38543

Rollercoaster Records, PO Box 18F, Chessington, Surrey; 01-397 8957

Rough Trade Records, 137 Blenheim Crescent, London W11; 01-727 5081

RSO Records, 67 Brook Street, London W1; 01-629 9121

Safari Records, 42 Manchester Street, London W1; 01-486 6141

Satril Records, Satril House, 444 Finchley Road, London NW2; 01-435 8063

Spartan Records, London Road, Wembley, Middlesex; 01-903 4753

Stiff Records, 9-11 Woodfield Road, London W9; 01-289 6221

Swan Song, 484 Kings Road, London SW10; 01-351 4151

Sweet Folk All, Shrewsbury Lane, Shooters Hill, London SW18; 01-854 4014

Trojan Recordings Ltd, 104 High Street, Harlesdon, London NW10; 01-961 4565

United Artists' Records, EMI House, Manchester Square, London W1; 01-486 4488

Virgin Records, 2-4 Vernon Yard, 119 Portobello Road, London W11; 01-727 8070

WEA Records, 20 Broadwick Street, London W1; 01-434 3232

Zoom Records, 45 Shandwick Place, Edinburgh; 031-229 3533

Trade Organisations and Associated Industry Bodies

Arts Council of Great Britain, 105 Piccadilly, London W1V 0AU; 01-629 9495

Association of Touring and Producing Managers, Suite 14-43, 18 Charing Cross Road, London WC2; 01-836 2133

Association of Professional Recording Studios Ltd, 23 Chestnut Avenue, Chorleywood, Hertfordshire WD3 4HA; 09237 72907

British Arts Festivals Association, 33 Rufford Road, Sherwood, Nottingham NG5 2NQ; 0602 61979

The British Association of Concert Agents, 12 Addison Park Mansions, Addison Gardens, London W14 0EB; 01-602 1998

British Copyright Council, 29 Berners Street, London W1; 01-580 5544

British Copyright Protection Association, 29-33 Berners Street, London W1; 01-580 5544

British Federation of Brass Bands, 47 Hull Road, York; 0904 59783

British Federation of Music Festivals, 106 Gloucester Place, London W1; 01-935 6371

British Federation of Folk Clubs, Cecil Sharpe House, 2 Regents Park Road, London NW1; 01-485 2206

British Institute of Recorded Sound, 29 Exhibition Road, London SW7; 01-589 6603

British Music Information Centre, 10 Stratford Place, London W1; 01-499 8567

British Phonographic Industry, Roxburghe House, 273-87 Regent Street, London W1R 8BN; 01-629 8642
     A non-profit-making body formed by manufacturers, producers and sellers of records and prerecorded tapes in the UK to protect and advance interests which are common to all of them. There are five grades of membership, A - E, with a heavy reliance upon the major companies which bear the brunt of the essential expenditure incurred by the association, and which have the largest say in its activities. Often described as the 'music industry watchdog'.

British Society for Electronic Music, 49 Deodar Road, London SW15; 01-870 4774

Campaign for Independent Broadcasting, 13 Ashwood House, London NW4; 01-203 0861

Central Entertainments Agents' Council, 64 Port Street, Evesham Worcestershire WR11 6AP; 0386 2819

Composers' Guild of Great Britain, 10 Stratford Place, London W1; 01-499 8567

Council of Brass Bands Association, 60 Whalley House, Wood Road, Manchester M16; 061-881 7895

Country Music Association (Great Britain), PO Box 2LG, London W1; 01-935 0413

Disc Jockeys' Federation of Great Britain, 196 Stapleton Hall Road, London N4 4QL; 01-341 2785

Disc Jockey Federation, 1 Low Farm Cottages, Drayton, Norwich NR8 6RR; 0603 860241

The English Folk Dance and Song Society, 2 Regents Park Road, London NW1 7AY; 01-485 2206

The Entertainment Agents' Association, 18 Charing Cross Road, London WC2; 01-240 1724

The Incorporated Society of Musicians, 10 Stratford Place, London W1; 01-629 4413

International Society for Contemporary Music, British Section, 105 Piccadilly, London W1V 0AU; 01-629 9495

Jazz Centre Society Limited, Third Floor, 35 Great Russell Street, London WC1; 01-580 8532

Mechanical Copyright Protection Society Limited, Elgar House, 380 Streatham High Road, London SW16; 01-769 4400
Whenever a record is sold, whether over the counter at a record shop or in a film or commercial, there is a 'mechanical' copyright due to the owner of the copyright — either the songwriter, or, if he has signed to a publishing company, then to that company. The MCPS collect the copyright (usually around 6¼ per cent of the recommended retail price) and distribute it to the relevant owner whose interests it represents. Publishers outnumber songwriters about 2:1 as members of the MCPS. It should be noted that most publishers keep 50 per cent of the royalty, whether mechanical or 'performance' — there are two separate amounts of royalties collectable from each song. For this, they will gladly take the administrative headaches involved in dealing with these bodies.

Musicians' Union, 60 Clapham Road, London SW9 0JJ; 01-582 5566

The Music Publishers' Association (also the owners of MCPS), Seventh Floor, Kingsway House, 103 Kingsway, London WC2B 6QX; 01-831 7591

The Music Trade Association, 5 Denmark Street, London WC2; 01-836 2059

National Federation of Music Societies, 1 Montague Street, London WC1; 01-580 4885

National Association of Disc Jockeys, PO Box 23, Hitchin, Hertfordshire; 0462 50918

Performing Rights Society Ltd, 29-33 Berners Street, London W1P 4AA; 01-580 5544
  Concerned with collecting all performing royalties for songs played live (via a venue licensing system), and broadcast on the radio or television. Royalties are paid to members — publishing companies or songwriters — on a quarterly basis. All venues — large or small, where music is played, whether recorded or live, should by law be licensed through the PRS, which is currently moving for record shops to be similarly licensed.

Songwriters' Guild of Great Britain, Ascot House, 52-3 Dean Street, London W1; 01-437 1554

Standing Conference for Amateur Music, 26 Bedford Square, London WC1; 01-636 4066